JANE'S POCKET BOOK OF PISTOLS AND SUB-MACHINE GUNS

JANE'S POCKET BOOK OF PISTOLS AND SUB-MACHINE GUNS

Edited by Denis Archer

MACDONALD AND JANE'S

FIRST PUBLISHED 1976

COPYRIGHT © DENIS ARCHER   1976

ISBN 0354 01013 1 (PVC EDITION)
ISBN 0354 01012 3 (LIBRARY EDITION)

This edition is not available for sale in the United States, its
dependencies, the Philippine Islands or the Dominion of
Canada.

Printed in England by
Netherwood Dalton & Co. Ltd., Huddersfield

PUBLISHED BY MACDONALD AND JANE'S PUBLISHERS
LIMITED
PAULTON HOUSE, 8 SHEPHERDESS WALK, LONDON N1
7LW

CONTENTS

FOREWORD

In common with other pocket books in this series this small volume is designed to meet the needs of those who require a readily-portable digest of weapon information or for whose purposes *Jane's Infantry Weapons* with its wider and more detailed coverage is inappropriate.

This volume is concerned with military pistols and sub-machine guns: the other principal small-calibre weapons, rifles and machine guns, are dealt with in a companion volume. The four categories could not be accommodated in a single pocket book without undesirable compression; and the division of the two groups is a natural one, there being much in common between pistols and sub-machine guns and between rifles and light machine guns, at least, whereas there are substantial differences between the two groups.

Some notes on the scope, contents and arrangement of the book are appended for the benefit of those who read the forewords of books. It is hoped that the contents list, layout and index will cater adequately for the needs of those who do not

Scope

In selecting weapons for inclusion I have sought, first, to cover all pistols and sub-machine guns known or believed to be currently officially in service with regular armed forces or reserve forces; secondly, to include those officially obsolescent or obsolete weapons which are excluded from the first category but may nevertheless still be encountered frequently because they are used by irregular forces or, unofficially, in regular forces; and thirdly to cover a representative selection of commercially available weapons which are similar to those used by the military and either are or may be used by police or para-military organisations.

Pistols, being portable, generally durable and not infrequently objects of sentimental attachment, are more likely than most weapons to remain in service beyond the date of their official withdrawal; and those that are withdrawn, often having been little used in service, are likely to be easy to sell on the second-hand arms market. Because of this it is quite likely that weapons of considerable age will be encountered from time to time; and although in selecting obsolescent and obsolete weapons for inclusion I have endeavoured to include those that are still in fairly widespread use, it is quite likely that my arbitrary choice does not coincide with that which another might make.

Sub-machine guns have a shorter history than pistols and are less noted for their ability to inspire affection; but their distribution is otherwise governed by influences similar to those just described for pistols. Generally similar criteria have therefore been used in making the selection.

Status

For most weapons some indication of present status is given. In this context 'present' covers a period extending roughly from the Autumn of 1975 to the Spring of 1976; but news travels slowly in some channels and some of the information may be older than these dates suggest.

Data

In order to keep entries reasonably short I have confined the tabulated data for the weapons to a few significant characteristics. Muzzle velocities and energies have been omitted on the grounds that what matters most in this region is the practical effective range of the weapon: rates of fire, on the other hand, are included. Dimensions have been limited to major items such as weapon length, barrel length and weight, expressed (except for calibres which are given in imperial or metric units according to custom) only in metric units and to the nearest 0.5 centimetre in length and 0.1 kilogram in weight. This last decision may surprise some readers; but my belief is that anyone who is really interested in greater accuracy than this will probably also be interested in many other details for which there is insufficient room in a work of this size. Fuller information on most weapons can, of course, be obtained from *Jane's Infantry Weapons*.

In the weapon data summaries, manufacturers' names are given in shortened form. Fuller information is contained in the section dealing with weapon manufacture.

Arrangement

Weapon descriptions have been grouped in four sections, dealing with revolver pistols, self-loading or automatic pistols, machine pistols and sub-machine guns, in that order. Within each section the entries for individual weapons have been arranged in ascending order of calibre, in alphabetical order of country of origin within each calibre division, and roughly in chronological order within each country subdivision. Where, as often happens, a weapon is made in different versions to fire ammunition of two or more different calibres, one of the versions — usually that most frequently encountered — is selected for description in reasonable detail and the others are in general covered by brief notes and cross-references in the appropriate calibre division of the book.

Where a weapon is or has been manufactured under licence in a country other than its country of origin a separate entry for the licence-built version is included only if it is noticeably different from the original or otherwise of special importance. Otherwise the licence arrangements are referred to in the main entry or in the weapon manufacture section of the book.

Denis Archer

INTRODUCTION

Although weapons of several different types are described on the following pages, the principal discontinuity in the sequence of descriptions is between the two fundamentally different types of pistol, the revolver and the self-loading or 'automatic' pistol. The essential difference is that, for the revolver, all the operations of loading, positioning and firing the rounds and subsequently removing the spent cases from the weapon are performed manually by the firer: for all the other weapons described in this book some of these operations are performed by mechanisms which are powered, directly or indirectly, by the propellant charge.

Revolvers

In the revolver pistol — which is the correct, but rarely-used, name of the weapon — the rounds are contained in a rotatable cylinder which is indexed round by one cartridge position between each shot, thus presenting a fresh cartridge to be struck by the hammer. The indexing mechanism is linked to the cocking mechanism, and the cylinder rotates as the hammer moves back into the cocked position.

There are two distinct types of trigger and hammer operation; and in what is called double-action operation the hammer is moved backwards (and the cylinder indexed into its new position) by pressure on the trigger. Considerable pressure is required, because the hammer is spring-loaded, and it must be maintained until the hammer is as far back as it will go. This constitutes the first part of the double action: further pressure on the trigger operates a trip mechanism which allows the hammer to be driven forward by its spring and to fire the round. With this type of mechanism the first

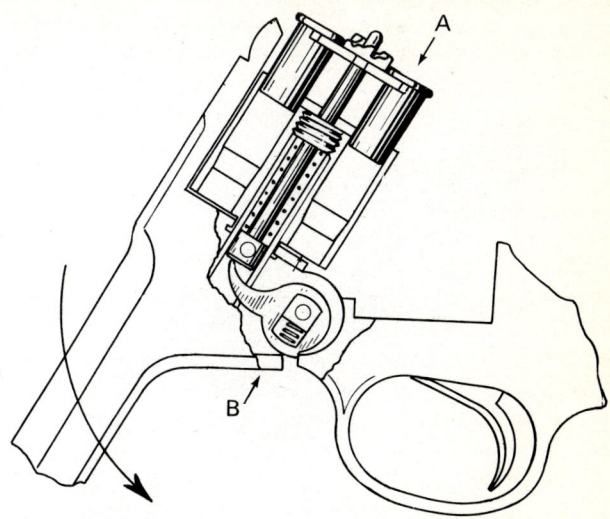

Top-breaking revolver mechanism showing case extraction.

and second parts of the double action are not separated: both are carried out by a single long movement of the trigger.

In a single-action pistol mechanism, on the other hand, the hammer has a stable cocked position into which it is moved by a manual operation, not involving the trigger and

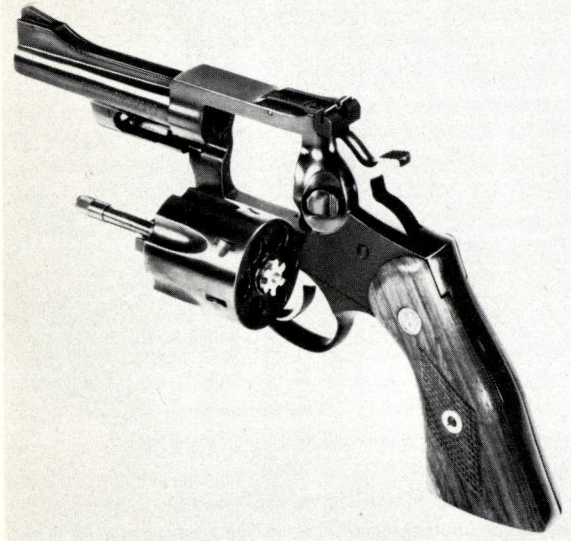

This Ruger Security Six revolver has a side-loading cylinder.

usually performed by the firer's thumb, which also indexes the cylinder into its new position. When cocked in this way the gun can be fired by a trigger pressure which is much smaller than that required for double-action operation; and in many double-action pistols a stable cocked hammer position is available so that the weapon can be thumb-cocked and fired by single trigger action if required.

Double-action firing is the quicker of the two methods (if the complete cycle is considered) and has the advantage of involving a smaller risk of accidental discharge; but the high trigger pressure required makes it difficult to maintain a steady aim.

Although not all self-loading pistols have accessible hammers, the distinction between single-action and double-action operation applies to them as well as to revolvers. Another feature that is common to some revolvers and some self-loading pistols with accessible hammers is a second, intermediate or 'half-cock' stable position for the hammer. It is a 'safe' position because the weapon cannot be fired until the hammer is moved back to the fully-cocked position.

Revolvers are mechanically simple, robust and reliable and capable of being fired with considerable accuracy. Because they are bulky and can fire only a few rounds before having to be rather laboriously reloaded, they are not widely used by the military. They are, however, popular with police and other forces where reliability is a more important consideration than firepower.

Self-loading Pistols

As already noted, in self-loading pistols — or 'automatics' as they are widely if slightly inaccurately known — the weapon mechanisms are to some extent powered by the propellant charge. This is possible because the propellant gases driving the bullet up the barrel of a pistol are also exerting the same pressure in all other directions; and while the results of the effective pressures at right-angles to the barrel axis largely cancel one another out because of the symmetry of the system, the forward momentum imparted to the bullet must, since the system is a closed one, be matched by an equal momentum imparted to something else in the opposite direction.

This something else may be described as the recoiling mass and, since momentum is the product of mass and velocity, its recoil velocity will be inversely proportional to its mass. It is also worth noting that the kinetic energy of a moving body is proportional to the product of its mass and the square of its velocity; with the result that, in any given set of circumstances, an increase in the recoiling mass will result in a decrease in the amount of kinetic energy that it acquires (because its velocity will be less) and hence an increase in the kinetic energy imparted to the bullet.

Recoil Operation

In a practical magazine-fed system, assuming that the recoiling mass is to perform some useful mechanical function, the extremes of choice of recoiling mass available are defined by two requirements. First, the mechanism must at least be able to extract the spent cartridge case and replace it by a new round: this means that at some stage in the recoil cycle the breech must open and the breech block be separated from the breech by more than the length of a round, so that on its return journey it can strip a fresh round

from the magazine and insert it in the chamber. Secondly, because the gas pressure in the barrel is very high while the bullet remains in the barrel, it is important that the breech should remain closed (though not necessarily locked) until after the bullet has emerged from the muzzle, otherwise there will be a wasteful and dangerous blast of gas from the breech.

In a typical system using a heavy recoiling mass, the breech remains closed by a mechanical lock between the barrel and the breech block until it is to start to open the breech. The locked assembly recoils against the pressure of a spring which is fixed to the main body of the weapon. At a carefully selected point on the recoil path, the mechanical lock is released and the barrel brought to rest in relation to the weapon body: the breech block (and anything attached to it) continues rearwards against the spring pressure, withdrawing the spent case from the chamber and ejecting it. The withdrawal action will in general be aided by the residual gas pressure in the barrel; but the mechanism must be designed so that the cartridge case is not clear of the breech until the gas pressure has dropped to a safe level.

What happens next depends on the particular mechanism employed, but at some stage in the sequence of operations the breech block will be driven forward by the recoil spring and strip a round from the magazine. It then feeds the round into the chamber and, as it pushes it home, drives the barrel forward and re-engages the breech locking mechanism.

A system operating in this way is known as a 'short recoil' system, to distinguish it from one in which the barrel and breech block remain locked until they have recoiled to the maximum distance, the barrel then being returned in

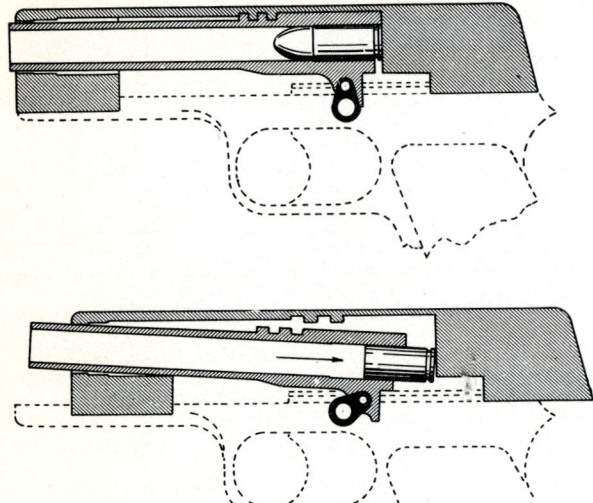

Colt M1911 locking system. The barrel is disengaged from the slide by a pivoting link.

advance of the breech block. Long recoil systems are rare.

Blowback Operation

Short recoil systems have several advantages over competing systems: the heavy recoiling mass absorbs little energy from the propellant; the breech is not opened until the barrel pressure is quite low so that there is little fouling and it is not necessary to use a straight-sided cartridge; and a high proportion of the total recoil energy is dissipated in the recoil mechanism, thus reducing the weapon's 'kick'. Their disadvantage is that the mechanism must be well made to function satisfactorily and must therefore be relatively expensive.

An alternative is what is usually called a 'blowback' system in which, typically, the breech is not locked at all and the recoiling mass is the cartridge case and the breech block, plus whatever else may be attached to it. It is at once apparent that such a system can perform the same functions as a short recoil system but without the elaboration of the unlocking and locking processes. It is worth noting, also, that although the terms 'blowback' and 'recoil' are commonly used in such a way as to suggest that there is a difference in principle between the systems to which they are applied, both arrangements are in fact strictly recoil-operated.

In a pure blowback system, the breech starts to open as soon as the round is fired: means must therefore be found to prevent the spent case from being withdrawn from the breech before the gas pressure has fallen to a safe level. This imposes such requirements as straight sides to the cartridge case and some limitation on the power of the cartridge that can be used.

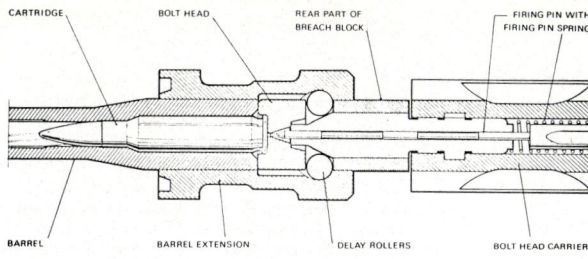

CARTRIDGE   BOLT HEAD   REAR PART OF BREACH BLOCK   FIRING PIN WITH FIRING PIN SPRING

BARREL   BARREL EXTENSION   DELAY ROLLERS   BOLT HEAD CARRIER

Rifle loaded, ready to fire

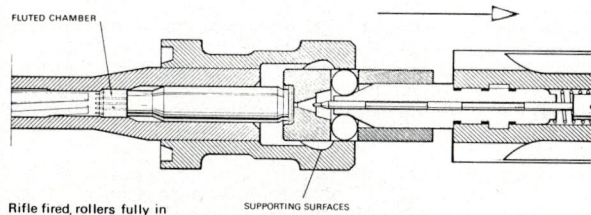

FLUTED CHAMBER

Rifle fired, rollers fully in   SUPPORTING SURFACES

Heckler and Koch delayed blowback system for the G3 rifle. Delay is provided by the need to unlock the delay rollers before the breech can open fully.

Delayed Blowback

Two other ways in which the complete opening of the breech can be delayed in a blowback system are by increasing the mass, and hence the inertia, of the recoiling parts and by strengthening the recoil spring. The first method is of limited usefulness in pistols but is much used in sub-machine guns where the added weight can more readily be tolerated: the second method is also limited in application because too strong a spring will make the action harsh and give rise to excessive wear.

A third method is to insert a mechanical delay mechanism in the recoil path — some form of locking mechanism that can be forced by the rearward pressure — so that the rapid blowback movement does not start immediately. Arrangements of this sort are widely used in pistol mechanisms whereas most sub-machine guns have pure blowback mechanisms.

It should be noted that a delayed blowback system is intermediate between a pure blowback and a short recoil system. While the mechanical delay is operating some of the recoil energy is communicated to the pistol as a whole.

Blowback systems are on the whole simpler and cheaper than short recoil systems — which is why they are so widely used for sub-machine guns. In relation to recoil operation, however, they have the disadvantages of a greater tendency to fouling and the cartridge limitations mentioned earlier.

Firing Mechanisms

With any of the self-loading systems described above several different kinds of firing system can be associated. In the least-automated of these the end of the cycle occurs with the breech closed and a round in the chamber whereafter the weapon is fired by a double-action manual system (possibly with the option of hand-cocked single action) similar to that of a revolver.

Moving in the direction of increasing automation, the next stage is one in which the breech is closed as before but the hammer (or its equivalent) is cocked so that the weapon can be fired with a single trigger action. In the next stage the cycle ends with the breech open and the mechanism to the rear, held there by the trigger mechanism: when the trigger is pressed the mechanism goes forward, chambers a round and fires it. The actual firing mechanism in this system can take different forms which will be considered below in the context of sub-machine gun mechanisms: the only further point to be made here is that this system lends itself readily to a sustained automatic fire arrangement.

Machine Pistols

A pistol (revolver or self-loading) can be conveniently defined as a short-range firearm which is normally fired using only one hand. A sub-machine gun is also a short-range weapon which commonly fires the same ammunition as a pistol but which is characterised by a somewhat greater effective range, a generally larger capability for sustained fire and by the need to use two hands for its satisfactory operation.

An intermediate type of weapon is the machine pistol which can be aimed and fired with one hand but which is fitted with a folding stock to enable it to be used two-handed and which is rather better suited to automatic operation than the average self-loading pistol. There are no firm definitions in this area, however; some modern sub-machine guns are very light and compact and many pistols can be used with

shoulder stocks. Finally the distinctions are linguistically easier in English than in some other languages.

Sub-machine Guns

As already noted, simple blowback action is commonly used with sub-machine guns: in the larger weapon, however, it is possible to introduce some system refinements which are difficult or impossible within the small compass of the pistol. The possibility of using a relatively massive bolt to put more inertia into the blowback system has already been mentioned; and a refinement of this is the 'wrap-around' bolt which in its forward position encloses a large part of the barrel, the firing pin being located almost at the rear end of the bolt. The bolt is slotted for cartridge case ejection and for chambering the new round.

An arrangement of this kind has the advantages of minimising the space required for the mechanism behind the breech and of inhibiting the escape of gas in the direction of the firer. With suitable design it can also help to keep dirt out of the mechanism by blocking the ejection port when not in use.

Advanced Primer Ignition

In a wrap-around arrangement it is convenient if the cartridge is fired by a fixed firing pin on the bolt face; and indeed fixed firing pins have been a feature of some sub-machine gun designs from the earliest days although they are not universally used: some SMG fire from a closed breech position with a single-action trigger and others, firing from an open breech, have a firing pin which is tripped as the

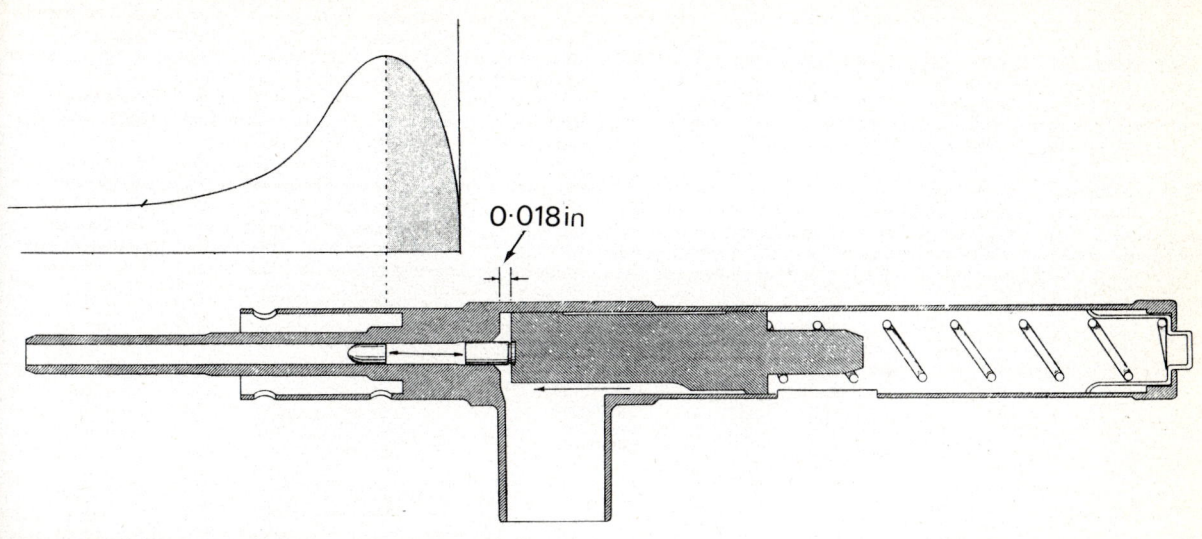

0·018 in

Advanced primer ignition on the Sten gun. At maximum pressure there is still
nearly half a millimetre clearance between the bolt face and the chamber face.

mechanism closes the breech.

With a fixed firing pin, however, it is possible to use an advanced primer ignition system in which the cartridge is fired while it is still moving forwards into the chamber. The result of this is that some of the recoil energy from the firing process is used up in checking the forward movement of the bolt thus achieving the required delay in the re-opening of the breech by yet another method.

Gas Operation

All blowback systems are subject to a limitation on the power of the cartridge for which they can be satisfactorily designed; and all the blowback and recoil systems discussed above have the disadvantage that they cannot by any simple means be adjusted to vary the rate at which the mechanism operates or to increase the power in the system to overcome the effects of dirt or cold on the operation of the weapon.

To overcome these difficulties the 'gas-operated' system was developed for automatic weapons and is widely used in automatic rifles and light machine guns. In such a system, propellant gases are tapped from the barrel and are used to operate the self-loading mechanism.

One or two gas-operated weapons, derived from what are basically automatic rifles, are sometimes classified as sub-machine guns; but since they use ammunition which is appropriate to a rifle rather than to a pistol and are therefore not strictly short-range weapons they have not been included among the entries in this book.

REVOLVER PISTOLS

(FRANCE)

This compact double-action revolver is available in three different barrel lengths and can fire .38 Special ammunition as well as the .357 Magnum round. It has a 6-shot cylinder which swings sideways for reloading.

Ammunition: .357 Magnum (or .38 Special)
Operation: Double-action or single-action
Cylinder: 6-chamber
Sights: Blade foresight; notch rear
Length: 19.5 cm, 20.5 cm or 23.5 cm for 6.5 cm, 7.5 cm or 10 cm barrels
Weight: about 0.9 kg according to barrel
Manufacturer: Manurhin
Status: In service with the French Army and security forces.

0.357 in MAGNUM COMMERCIAL REVOLVERS

Numerous revolvers are made, notably by US manufacturers, for use by law enforcement agencies and for sale to the general public. Such revolvers are not military weapons in the ordinary sense of the term; but many of them are made to standards similar to those laid down by the military and they are not infrequently encountered in internal security, para-military or military use. Popular calibres for such weapons are .357 in, .38 in and .45 in.

Among European revolver manufacturers a well-known maker of commercially-available weapons is Astra in Spain;

and some of their .357 Magnum revolvers have been encountered in circumstances of the kind just described.

Several American manufacturers make revolvers in the .357 Magnum calibre and some examples are illustrated here. Since these weapons are designed using imperial measures an exception to the general rule of this book has been made in favour of specifying the barrel lengths in their designed values rather than in metric approximations. All the weapons are 6-shot revolvers.

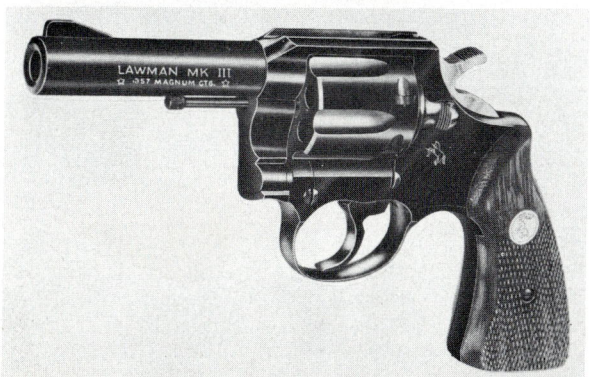

Colt Mk III Lawman. Made with 2in or 4in barrels.

Smith & Wesson M28 Highway Patrolman. 4in or 6in barrels.

(BELGIUM)

This new weapon, the first revolver to be designed by FN, is of conventional design with a five-chamber side-loading cylinder. Primarily intended for use with the 0.38 in Special cartridge, it will also accept the 0.38 in Smith and Wesson, and a version with cylinders chambered for the 9 mm Parabellum is planned.

Manufacturer: FN
Status: Development.

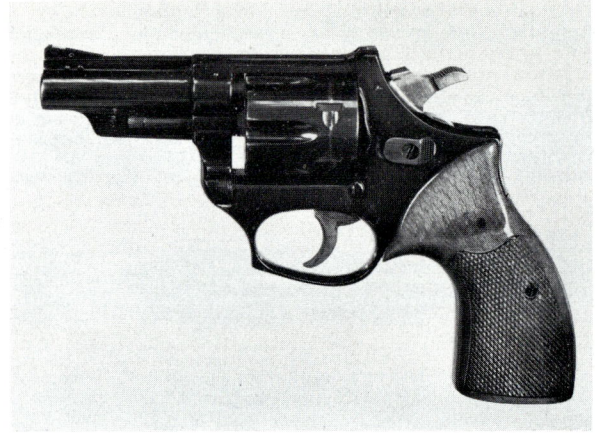

FN 0.38in Revolver.

9 mm FN REVOLVER

As noted in the entry for the 0.38 in FN revolver, a version to accept the 9 mm Parabellum cartridge is planned.

Manufacturer: FN
Status: Development.

0.38 in NEW NAMBU REVOLVER MODEL 60

This revolver is basically similar to the Smith and Wesson weapon of the same calibre. It has been the Japanese police pistol since 1961 and is also issued to the Japanese Maritime Safety Guard.

Ammunition: .38 Special
Operation: Manual revolver; single-action or double-action
Feed: 5-chamber cylinder
Sights: Blade foresight; notch rear
Rate of fire: 15 rounds/min
Effective range: 40 m
Total length: 19.5 cm (barrel 7.5 cm)
Weight: 0.7 kg
Date introduced: 1961 (police)
Manufacturer: Shin Chuo Kogyo Co.
Status: Production. Mainly police use. At least 70,000 sold.

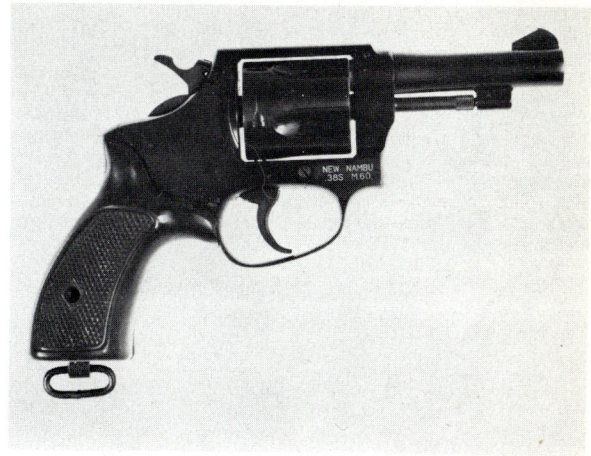

New Nambu Model 60 revolver.

This weapon was introduced in the British Army to meet the need for a revolver smaller than the .455 Webley and remained in service in various versions from 1932 until the last version was declared obsolete in 1963. The principal versions were the single/double-action No 2 Mk 1, the double-action Mk 1* and the short-lived double-action Mk 1** with no hammer safety stop. All these weapons were strictly military revolvers and were made by or under the direction of RSAF Enfield. They are no longer manufactured and no longer in British Army service; but very many of them are still in service in former British dependencies and elsewhere.

Data will be found in the entry for the Webley Mk IV.

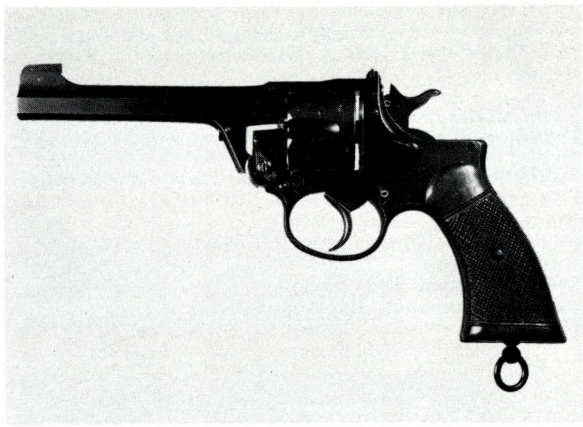

Pistol Revolver .38 No 2 Mk 1 *(RSAF)*.

0.38 in WEBLEY MK IV PISTOL REVOLVER   (UK)

The basis of the .38 in No 2 Pistol Revolver development was the Webley Mark IV which was virtually identical with the No 2 Mk 1, was issued in 1943 to supplement the standard issue and is still made as a commercial weapon.

The following data are representative both of the series of Enfield .38 revolvers and of the Webley Mk IV.

Ammunition: .380 SAA Ball; .380 Revolver; .38 Smith and Wesson, .38 Webley
Operation: Single/double-action (Mk IV and Mk 1), double-action (Mk 1* and Mk 1**) top-breaking revolver
Feed: 6-chamber cylinder
Sights: Blade foresight; U-notch rear
Rate of fire: 24 rounds/min
Effective range: 30 m
Total length: 26 cm (barrel 12.5 cm)
Weight: 0.8 kg
Date introduced: 1932
Manufacturers: RSAF with wartime support from Albion Motors and Singer Sewing Machine Company. Mk IV manufactured by Webley and Scott.
Status: Mk IV only still produced. All types in scattered service but none is now an official British Army weapon.

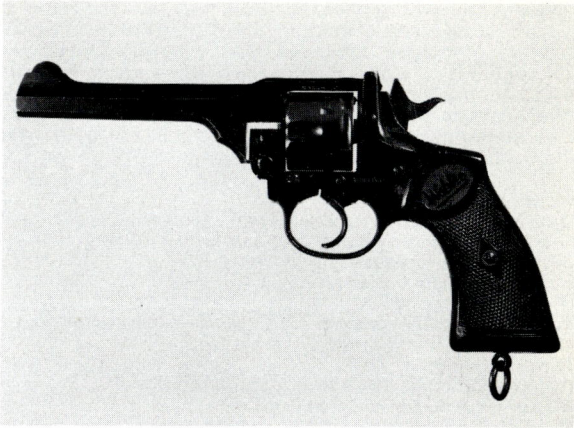

Webley Mk IV revolver *(RSAF)*.

23

0.38 in SMITH AND WESSON PISTOL REVOLVER NO. 2

This pistol was purchased from the USA for issue to British forces. It was manufactured from 1940 to 1945, during which time some 890,000 were produced; and although it is no longer in official use there are still a great many about. A six-chambered version of the Smith and Wesson Regulation Police Model, it fired a .380 round and was often known as the 38/200, the latter figure referring to the bullet weight.

Ammunition: 38/200
Operation: Single or double-action revolver
Feed: 6-chamber cylinder with swing-out loading
Sights: Blade foresight; notch rear
Rate of fire: 24 rounds/min
Effective range: 40 m
Total length: 26 cm with 12.5 cm (5 inch) barrel. Some 4 inch and 6 inch barrels were made.
Weight: 0.9 kg
Date introduced: 1940 in British service
Manufacturer: Smith and Wesson
Status: Made only during Second World War. See text.

Smith & Wesson Pistol Revolver No 2 *(RMCS)*.

0.38 in US COMMERCIAL REVOLVERS

Illustrated here are some typical US commercially-produced revolvers chambered for .38-in calibre ammunition. The notes in the corresponding entry for .357-in calibre are applicable here also. All are 6-shot revolvers except the Smith and Wesson 'Airweight' models which have 5-round cylinders.

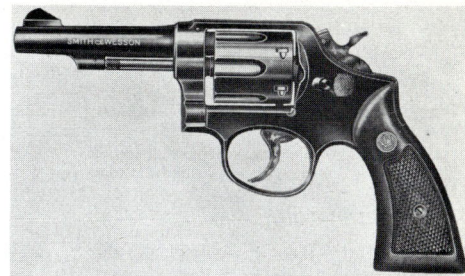

Smith & Wesson M10 Military and Police. Choice of 2, 4, 5 or 6-inch barrels.

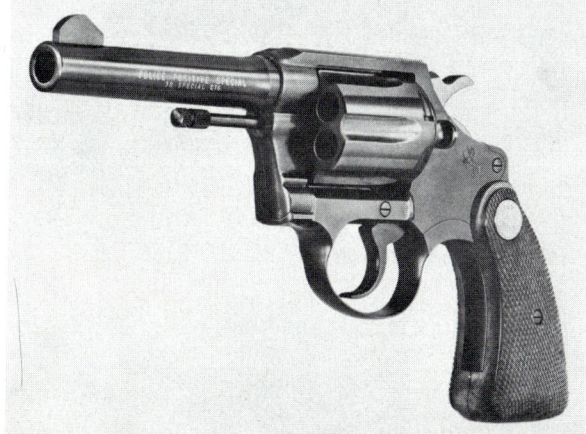

Colt Police Positive Special. 2in. or 4in. barrels.

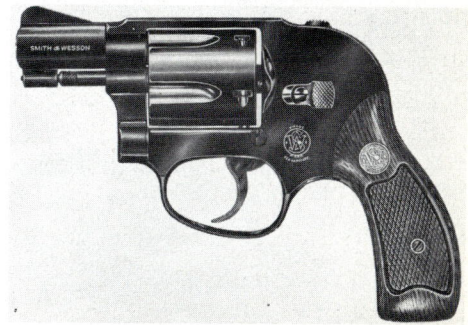

Smith & Wesson M38 Bodyguard 'Airweight' with 2-inch barrel and 5-round cylinder.

Although it has long since been withdrawn from British military service the Pistol Webley .455 is a popular weapon which may still be found in service in parts of the former British Empire. Many marks were produced, differing in minor detail, and all were top-breaking revolvers locked by a heavy stirrup and barrel catch. Early models had 4 inch (102 mm) barrels but from 1905 onwards 6 inch (152 mm) barrels were introduced. Data below relate to the final (Mk 6) model which had a square grip: all earlier marks had the "bird's head" grip.

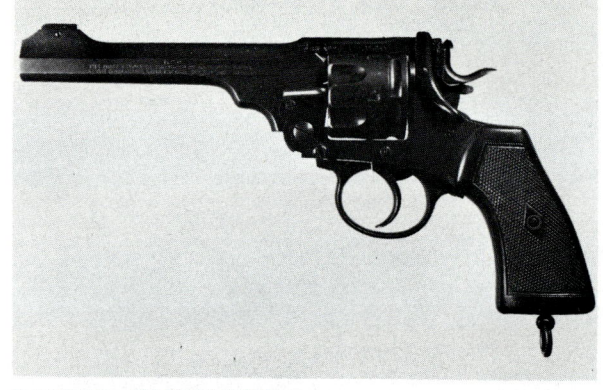

Pistol, Webley, 455 Mark 1 *(RSAF)*.

DATA (Pistol Revolver No 1 Mk 6)
Ammunition: .455 SAA Ball
Operation: Top-breaking revolver
Feed: 6-chamber cylinder
Sights: Blade foresight; notch rear
Rate of fire: 24 rounds/min
Effective range: 50 m
Length: 28.5 cm (barrel 15 cm)
Weight: 1.1 kg
Date introduced: (Mark 1) 1894
Manufacturer: Webley and Scott
Status: No longer manufactured. In scattered service (see text).

SELF-LOADING PISTOLS

For several years the French firm of Manurhin has manufactured Walther pistols under licence from the German company. Current production includes the PP in .22 LR which is illustrated here. Details will be found in the corresponding German entry.

.22LR Manurhin PP *(RSAF)*.

0.22 in LUGER PISTOL

(GERMANY — BRD)

Among many variants of the Luger pistol were some kit-converted versions in .22LR calibre. The best-known kit was supplied by Erma in Germany but all these versions are only rarely encountered.

Other information on Luger weapons will be found in the 9 mm entry.

0.22 in WALTHER PP AND PPK PISTOLS

Some of the German-produced PP and PPK pistols have been made by Walther in .22LR calibre but more have been made in 7.65 mm and 9 mm calibres. The .22LR version has also been made by Manurhin in France. Details of the weapons will be found in the entry for the 7.65 mm versions.

0.22 in HECKLER AND KOCH HK4 PISTOL

This is one of four versions of the HK4 weapon, the others being in 6.35 mm, 7.65 mm and 9 mm calibre. General details will be found in the 9 mm entry: those appropriate to the .22 version are the use of the .22LR (.22LfB) ammunition and a 10-round detachable box magazine in place of the the 8-round box of the 9 mm version. The 6.35 mm (.25ACP) version also has a 10-round magazine.

29

(SWITZERLAND)

SIG 210 is the general designation of a series of pistols all of which were made primarily to fire either 9 mm or 7.65 mm Parabellum ammunition but which can also be converted to fire the .22LR round. Model 49 is the Swiss Army designation of the SIG 210-2 pistol in 9 mm calibre. A conversion kit for .22LR comprises a barrel and associated return spring, a slide and a magazine all of which are easily fitted, so that for military training purposes the cheaper and more convenient .22 ammunition can be used without difficulty.

Details of the larger-calibre weapons, some of which are now in service with Swiss and Danish forces, will be found under the 9 mm heading. Characteristics of the .22 version are similar except for a slight reduction (about 50 grams) in weight.

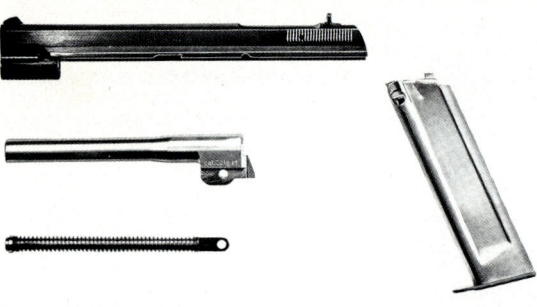

22LR conversion kit for P210.

7.62 mm TYPES 51 AND 54 (CHINA)

This is the standard Chinese Army pistol and is a direct copy of the Russian Tokarev TTM 1933 pistol. It may be distinguished from the Russian and Polish pistols of the same pattern by the uniformly narrow instead of alternately wide and narrow vertical serrations on the slide; and from the Hungarian 48M and Yugoslavian M57 by the Chinese markings in the receiver or slide and the absence of the Yugoslavian type number or Hungarian star wheatsheaf and hammer emblem.

Although the Chinese refer to TTM copies as Type 51 or Type 54 no difference between pistols so described is known.

Ammunition: 7.62 mm P cartridge or 7.63 mm Mauser
Operation: Recoil, semi-automatic
Magazine: 8-round box
Sights: Blade foresight; notch rear
Rate of fire: 35 rounds/min
Effective range: 50 m
Total length: 19.5 cm (barrel 11.5 cm)
Weight: 0.9 kg
Manufacturer: State factories
Status: In service

Type 51 pistol *(RSAF)*.

This pistol fires the Czech 7.62 mm M48 round which has the same dimensions as the Mauser 7.63 mm round and the Soviet Type P pistol cartridge (which can be fired by the M52) but has a larger propellant charge. Probably for this reason the pistol has been designed with an extremely strong, but elaborate and expensive, roller locking system. When used with the Czech ammunition it has a heavy recoil and pronounced muzzle blast.

Versions of the pistol have been made in 9 mm calibre for Swiss and Egyptian trials but neither was put into production. In its 7.62 mm standard version the weapon is still in limited service.

M52 pistol *(RMCS)*.

Ammunition: 7.62 mm M48 or Soviet Type P
Operation: Recoil-operated self-loading single action
Magazine: 8-round detachable box
Sights: Blade foresight; U-notch rear
Effective range: 60 m
Total length: 21 cm (barrel 12 cm)
Weight: 1 kg
Manufacturer: Uherskybrod Ordnance Factory
Status: In widely scattered but limited service including the Czech Army where it is being replaced by the Vz61 and Wz63 machine pistols.

7.62 mm MODEL 48 PISTOL   (HUNGARY)

This is the Hungarian version of the Russian Tokarev TT-33 pistol in the same calibre. It differs from the Russian weapon only in crest on the grip, which is a wreathed star, wheatsheaf and hammer, and in the uniform narrow vertical cuts on the slide. Common data for the weapons will be found in the TT-33 entry. Special data are given below.

A version chambered for the 9mm x 19 Parabellum cartridge and known as the Tokagypt is described separately.

Date introduced: 1948
Manufacturer: Hungarian State Arsenals
Status: In service in the Hungarian Army.

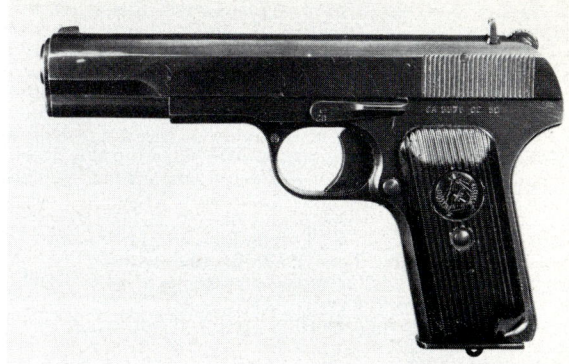

Hungarian M48 pistol *(RSAF)*.

Although the design of this weapon is based on the Russian Tokarev TT-33 it is shorter and bulkier than either the Russian weapon or the Chinese copies — Types 51 and 54. It may also be distinguished from these three weapons by the forward-sloping grip serrations at the rear end of the slide.

Internal differences are also numerous but the only one which impinges directly upon the user prevents the TT-33 from accepting a Type 68 magazine but permits the Type 68 to use a TT-33 magazine.

Ammunition: 7.62 mm x 25; Type P; 7.63 mm Mauser
Operation: Short recoil self-loading single action
Magazine: 8-round detachable box (see text)
Sights: Blade foresight; notch rear
Rate of fire: 32 rounds/min
Effective range: 50 m
Total length: 18.5 cm (barrel 11 cm)
Weight: 0.8 kg
Manufacturer: State factories
Status: In limited service with North Korean forces.

North Korean Type 68 pistol.

7.62 mm TOKAREV TT-33 PISTOL

(USSR)

Although this weapon has been replaced in the armies of the Warsaw Treaty countries by the Russian Makarov pistol, it is still used in Yugoslavia and in many Asian countries. It has been produced, as more or less exact copies, in China (PRC), Hungary, Poland and Yugoslavia. There was also a 9 mm x 19 (Parabellum) version made in Hungary and known as the Tokagypt because it was intended for Egyptian use. The TT-33 is a short recoil weapon using the Colt-Browning operating principle of the Colt Model 1911, the barrel being unlocked from the slide after the short recoil by a pivoted link which pulls it downwards.

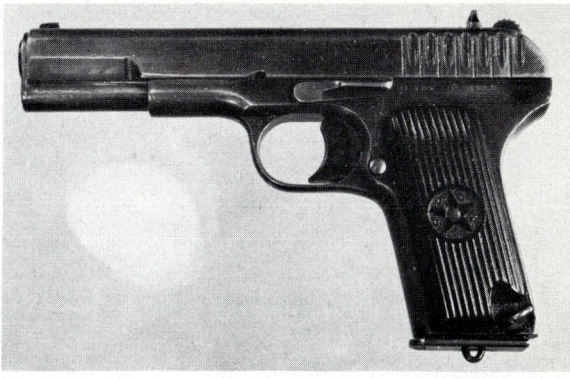

Tokarev TT 33.

Ammunition: 7.62 mm x 25 Type P
Operation: Short recoil, self-loading, single-action
Magazine: 8-round detachable box
Sights: Blade foresight; notch rear
Rate of fire: 32 rounds/min
Effective range: 50 m
Total length: 19.5 cm (barrel 11.5 cm)
Weight: 0.9 kg
Date introduced: 1933
Manufacturer: State factories
Status: No longer produced in Russia or in official service with Warsaw Treaty forces. See text.

First designed in 1894 this pistol was produced in various forms over a period of some forty years and was extensively used up to the end of the Second World War. Most were in 7.63 mm calibre but a few were made to fire 9 mm Parabellum ammunition. The Mauser's distinctive and somewhat awkard appearance results from the decision to mount the internal magazine forward of the trigger guard and the resultant reduction in the size of the butt compared with those of most other self-loading pistols.

The pistol fires from a closed, locked breech and operates on the short recoil principle with swinging block locking. All the early models are single-shot semi-automatic weapons and the data given below relate to these. The selective-fire versions produced in 1931 and 1932 are described separately.

Mauser M32 issued to the Waffen SS *(RSAF)*.

Ammunition: 7.63 mm Mauser
Operation: Short-recoil Semi-automatic
Magazine: 10-round internal, clip loaded. Some late models were modified to take detachable 10, 20 or 40-round box magazines and some of these were used by German forces.
Sights: Blade foresight. The standard rear sight was a tangent leaf and notch, but this was replaced by a simple notch in some later models.
Rate of fire: 24 rounds/min
Effective range: 50 m
Total length: 31 cm (with 14 cm standard barrel: a version with a 9.5 cm barrel was produced in 1920 and a few carbines with 30 cm barrels were made in the early days).
Weight: 1.2 kg
Date introduced: 1896
Manufacturer: Mauser
Status: No longer manufactured and no longer in regular service.

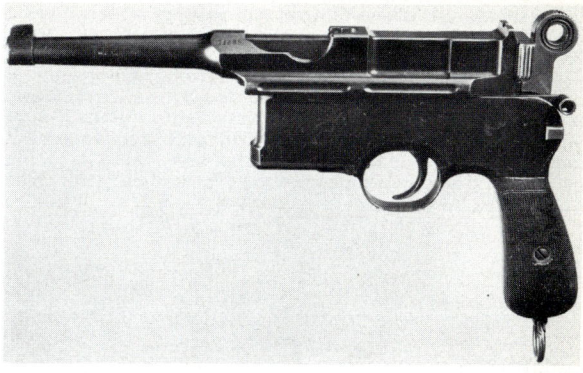

7.63mm Mauser M1895 pistol *(RSAF)*.

These variants of the Mauser self-loading principle were introduced partly to counteract the competition from Spanish rapid-fire pistols having an external appearance very similar to that of the Mauser. Two different designs of selective-fire pistol were produced, the differences relating to the selective-fire mechanism and the shape of the trigger and selector switch. The internal magazine arrangement was replaced by one that would accept detachable 10-round or 20-round box magazines but the clip-loading facility was retained as an option. A shoulder stock could be fitted.

In common with all such weapons the Schnellfeuer suffered from severe muzzle climb when firing fully automatic, making the value of all rounds after the first problematical.

Status: First introduced in 1931 these weapons are believed to have been used for military purposes only in Germany, China and Yugoslavia, all before or during the Second World War. No longer in regular service. No longer manufactured.

7.62 mm M57 PISTOL   (YUGOSLAVIA)

This is a copy of the Russian 7.62 mm Tokarev TT-33 pistol produced in Yugoslavia, It can be distinguished from pistols of Russian manufacture by the crest on the grip consisting of a star, a wheatsheaf and a hammer enclosed by a wreath. Otherwise the weapon is believed to be identical with the TT-33. It is still in service with Yugoslav forces.

(BELGIUM)

This pistol was manufactured by FN in versions using the 7.65 mm (.32ACP) and the 9 mm Short (.380ACP). It was a striker-fired, blowback-operated weapon having the return spring around the barrel. It had a grip safety, a manual safety and the Browning disconnector. Although designed in 1910 and marketed in 1912 it is still in production for sale to the USA.

Ammunition: 7.65 mm (.32ACP)
Operation: Blowback, semi-automatic
Magazine: 7-round detachable box
Sights: Blade foresight; notch rear
Rate of fire: 35 rounds/min
Effective range: 40 m
Total length: 15 cm (barrel 9 cm)
Weight: 0.6 kg
Date introduced: 1912
Manufacturer: FN
Status: Production. Not known to be in service with any regular military formation.

7.65mm Browning Model 1910 *(RSAF)*.

7.65 mm FN PISTOL

At the time of writing full details of this new pistol have not been released by the manufacturer, but it is known that it may be fired with either single or double-action initially and that the safety catch may be operated from either the left or right of the slide.

It is also known that FN are upgrading the 7.65 mm cartridge by a basic redesign of the bullet, the new version of which will have a truncated nose. The new bullet is expected to have stopping characteristics superior to those of the standard 7.65 mm ammunition.

Manufacturer: FN
Status: Nearing production.

FN 7.65mm pistol.

Designed primarily as an assassination weapon this pistol can be used either manually operated for single shots or as a self-loader. For maximum silencing the weapon fires from a locked breech, after which the bolt is manually unlocked and the slide retracted to extract the empty case. Alternatively, blowback operation can be selected but this is mechanically much noisier. In either case a muzzle silencer is applied in the form of a large bulbous attachment to the front of the receiver extending well forward of the muzzle. This comprises a wire mesh cylinder surrounded by an expanded metal sleeve and a series of rubber discs through which the bullet passes and which trap the gases. The result, in single-shot operation, is an extremely quiet weapon but with a low muzzle velocity and poor penetration. A unique 7.65 mm x 17 cartridge is used.

Chinese Type 64 silenced pistol with breech open.

Ammunition: 7.65 mm x 17 rimless
Operation: Manual single shot with rotating bolt locking or blowback semi-automatic
Magazine: 8-round box
Sights: Blade foresight; notch rear
Rate of fire: 32 rounds/min (semi-automatic)
Effective range: 35 m
Total length: 33 cm with silencer (barrel 12.5 cm)
Weight: 1.3 kg
Manufacturer: State factories
Status: In service.

7.65 mm Vz27 PISTOL   (CZECHOSLOVAKIA)

This self-loading pistol was made in large numbers before the Second World War and was adopted in slightly modified form by the German Army as the Pistol 27(t). Those pistols were marked 'Bohmische Waffenfabrik AG, Prague'. Postwar weapons were marked 'Narodny Podnik'. The Vz27 is a blowback-operated weapon of conventional design except that it has a detachable barrel which can be rotated off the receiver.

Ammunition: 7.65 mm (.32ACP)
Operation: Blowback semi-automatic
Magazine: 8-round detachable box
Sights: Blade foresight; notch rear
Rate of fire: 30 rounds/min
Effective range: 40 m
Total length: 16 cm (barrel 10 cm)
Weight: 0.7 kg
Manufacturer: Ceskoslovenska Zbrojovka
Status: Obsolescent and no longer in production.

Czech 7.65mm Vz27 pistol *(RSAF)*.

(CZECHOSLOVAKIA)

In many respects similar to the German Walther PP and PPK pistols this is a blowback-operated weapon with an external hammer and capable only of double-action operation. It is still carried by senior Czech officers but is not in general use. Pistols sold on the export market by Omnipol are marked Vz50.

Ammunition: 7.65 mm (.32ACP)
Operation: Blowback
Magazine: 8-round detachable box
Sights: Blade foresight; notch rear
Rate of fire: 35 rounds/min
Effective range: 40 m
Total length: 17.5 cm (barrel 9.5 cm)
Weight: 0.7 kg
Manufacturer: Ceskoslovenska Zbrojovka
Status: In very limited home service and no longer in production. Many exported.

Czech Vz50 *(RSAF)*.

7.65 mm MANURHIN PPK PISTOL (FRANCE)

This is the smaller of the two pistols currently in production, under licence from Walther, at Manurhin. Details of the PPK will be found in the corresponding German entry but an example of the licence-built weapon is illustrated here.

7.45 mm Maharkia PPK

Introduced in 1940 this is a double-action blowback weapon with the detachable magazine in the butt. It was not the first Mauser pistol to be configured thus: the 7.65 mm (or 6.35 mm) Model 1910 had a similar arrangement; and in both models the slide is held open when the last round has been fired, remains open when the magazine is removed but goes forward when an empty or loaded magazine is re-inserted, chambering a round in the latter instance. On some HSc models the hammer is almost totally enclosed but has a sufficient protrusion to enable the user to lower it on a loaded chamber: in other models even this protrusion is absent.

Ammunition: 7.65 mm (.32ACP). A 9 mm version called the HSv was developed but not adopted for military service.
Operation: Blowback semi-automatic
Magazine: 8-round detachable box
Sights: Blade foresight; notch rear
Rate of fire: 30 rounds/min
Effective range: 40 m
Total length: 16.5 cm (barrel 8.5 cm)
Weight: 0.6 kg
Date introduced: 1940
Manufacturer: Mauser
Status: Used during the Second World War mainly by the German Navy and Air Force. Currently in production for commercial sale and not known to be in regular military service.

7.65mm Mauser HSc with finger spur on the magazine.

7.65 mm LUGER PISTOL AND CARBINE

Although most Luger pistols are to be found in 9 mm calibre, the original design was for a 7.65 mm weapon. The change to 9 mm was made because most military authorities wanted more potent ammunition, but manufacture in 7.65 mm continued certainly until 1935 and possibly later. One version produced in this calibre was a carbine with a barrel just under twelve inches (300 mm) long and fitted with a shoulder stock. First produced in 1902 it is believed to have last been made in 1920.

Other information on Luger weapons will be found in the 9 mm entry.

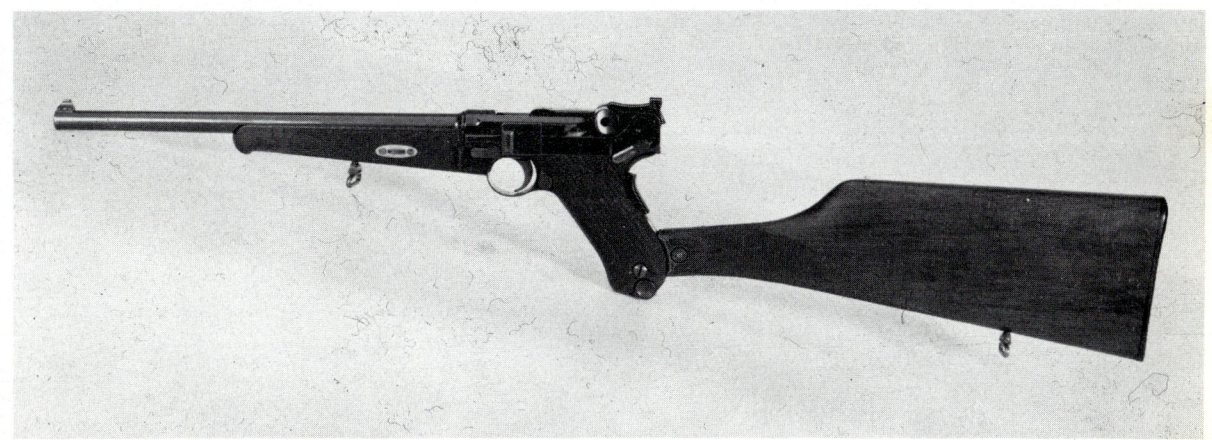

The carbine version of the 7.65mm Luger *(RMCS)*.

(GERMANY — BRD)

These two pistols were originally designed for police use, the PP (introduced 1929) to be carried on the uniform belt and the PPK (introduced 1931) for use as a concealed weapon. Basically 7.65 mm (.32ACP) designs, both were also made in 9 mm Short (.380ACP) and .22LR calibres. A few were also made in 6.35 mm (.25ACP). Both models are blowback operated with external hammers and double-action triggers: the PPK is smaller and lighter than the PP; the reduction being achieved by using a smaller magazine and a shorter barrel. The initials PP stand for Polizei Pistole and the K stands for Kriminal.

7.65mm Walther PPK pistol.

Ammunition: 7.65 mm (.32ACP). See text
Operation: Blowback with double-action trigger
Magazine: 8-round or 7-round (PPK) detachable box
Sights: Blade foresight; notch rear
Rate of fire: 30 rounds/min
Effective range: 40 m. Muzzle velocity of the PPK is about 3% lower than that of the PP
Total length: 17.5 cm or 15.5 cm (PPK). Barrel lengths 10 cm or 8.5 cm (PPK)
Weight: 0.7 kg or 0.6 kg (PPK)
Date introduced: PP in 1929; PPK in 1931
Manufacturer: Walther. Made under licence or copied in Hungary, Turkey and elsewhere.
Status: Production. Widely used during the Second World War and still in police use and with French, German, Hungarian and Turkish armed forces.

7.65mm Walther PP.

(GERMANY — BRD)

7.65 mm SAUER MODEL 1938(H) PISTOL

Produced for police work and as a pocket pistol in 6.35 mm, 7.65 mm and 9 mm (Short) calibre this weapon was adopted as a German substitute standard in 7.65 mm calibre and used by German tank forces and by the Luftwaffe in the Second World War.

The pistol is blowback-operated with a double-action trigger and can be cocked and fired by a long trigger pull. It can also be cocked to fire single-action by means of a lever, on the left of the grip, which can also be used to lower the cocked hammer under control.

Ammunition: 7.65 mm (.32ACP)
Operation: Blowback semi-automatic with single or double-action firing
Magazine: 8-round detachable box
Sights: Blade foresight; notch rear
Rate of fire: 24 rounds/min
Effective range: 30 m
Total length: 16 cm (barrel 8.5 cm)
Weight: 0.7 kg
Date introduced: 1938
Manufacturer: Sauer
Status: No longer manufactured or in regular military service.

7.65mm Sauer Model 38 pistol *(RSAF)*.

7.65 mm HECKLER AND KOCH HK4 PISTOL

This is one of four versions of the HK4 weapon, the others being in .22LR, 6.35 mm and 9 mm calibre. General details will be found in the 9 mm entry: those appropriate to the 7.65 mm version are the use of 7.65 mm (.32ACP) ammunition and a 9-round detachable box magazine in place of the 8-round box of the 9 mm version.

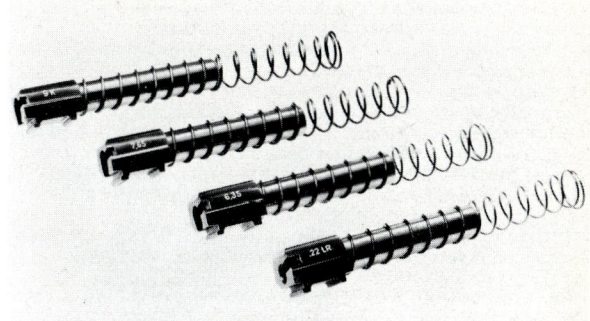

Alternative barrels and springs for the HK4.

This is basically a modified Browning blowback type of pistol which was adopted by the Hungarian Army in 1937 and is now no longer manufactured — but may still be encountered. Three versions may be identified — the standard 7.65 mm Hungarian Army model (itself an improved version of an earlier 1929 model), the same pistol chambered for 9 mm and a 7.65 mm version produced for the German Army during its occupation of Hungary in the Second World War. The German Army version had a manual safety in addition to the standard grip safety and was marked in German instead of Magyar.

The pistol was well made and, although a little heavy, was popular with the troops to whom it was issued.

Ammunition: 7.65 mm (.32ACP). See text
Operation: Blowback semi-automatic
Magazine: 7-round detachable box
Sights: Blade foresight; notch rear
Rate of fire: 28 rounds/min
Effective range: 40 m
Total length: 17.5 cm (barrel 10 cm)
Weight: 0.8 kg
Date introduced: 1937 (Hungarian Army version)
Manufacturer: Fegyvergyan
Status: Obsolescent and no longer made. Used by Hungarian Army from 1937 and by German Army in wartime. May still be encountered.

Hungarian M1937 pistol *(RSAF)*.

7.65 mm M48 PISTOL

This is a Hungarian copy of the German Walther PP pistol which differs from the original only in the arrangement of the loaded-chamber indicator. In the Hungarian version the indicator emerges from the left top side of the slide, over the chamber, instead of the rear.

The M49 was used by the Hungarian police forces. A 9 mm version was made for sale to Egypt but the few produced were sold commercially.

7.65mm version of the M48 *(RSAF)*.

This pistol is a version of the Beretta Model 1934 9 mm pistol designed to use the 7.65 mm (.32ACP) ammunition. It is a little lighter than the 9 mm version but in other respects has the same characteristics. It is not, however, a standard service weapon and was not made in large quantity. The 9 mm weapon is separately described.

7.65 mm NEW NAMBU MODEL 57B AUTOMATIC PISTOL   (JAPAN)

This is a self-loading, blowback-operated weapon, the design of which is based on Browning ideas. It has an external hammer and features a loaded-chamber indicator.

Ammunition: 7.65 mm (.32ACP)
Operation: Blowback-operated self-loading
Magazine: 8-round detachable box
Sights: Blade foresight; notch rear
Rate of fire: 24 rounds/min
Effective range: 40 m
Total length: 15 cm (barrel 9 cm)
Weight: 0.6 kg
Manufacturer: Shin Chuo Kogyo Co.

7.65mm New Nambu Model 57B.

This is essentially a copy of the 1900 Browning design. Stamped "1964 7.62" it nevertheless fires the 7.65 mm x 17 SR cartridge which is the American Colt .32ACP. It is blowback-operated and semi-automatic.

Two versions have been produced, one of which is designed for use with a silencer: to enable the silencer to be fitted the slide has been shortened and the resulting barrel projection threaded to accept the silencer.

Ammunition: 7.65 mm (.32ACP)
Operation: Blowback semi-automatic
Magazine: 7-round detachable box
Sights: Blade foresight; notch rear
Effective range: 30 m unsilenced
Length: 17 cm (barrel 10 cm)
Weight: 0.6 kg (unsilenced)
Date introduced: 1954
Manufacturer: State factories
Status: In limited service with North Korean forces.

Silenced and unsilenced North Korean Type 64 pistols.

7.65 mm MODEL 06/29 PISTOL

(SWITZERLAND)

Switzerland was the first country to adopt the Luger for military use and had 3000 of the 7.65 mm Model 1900 made for them by DWM in that year plus a further 2000 for commercial sale. Subsequently they acquired quantities of the 'new' Model 1906 in the same calibre for military and police use. In 1924 manufacture of a slightly modified copy of the Model 1906 was started at Waffenfabrik, Berne, and further modifications — to the grip shape and safety — were made in 1929, the resultant pistol being designated Mod 00-06-29. It was in first line service until 1949 but was then relegated to reserve units. Details will be found in the 7.65 mm Luger entry.

Manufacturer: Waffenfabrik, Bern
Status: No longer made. Reserve service only.

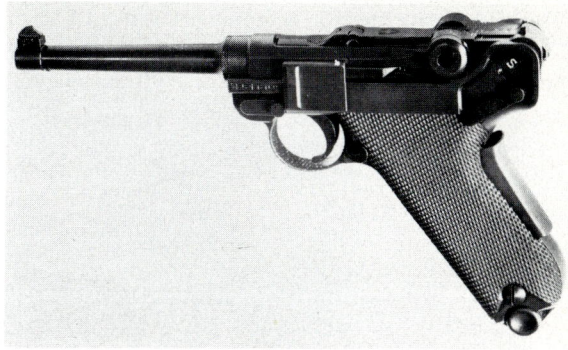

Swiss-made 06/29 version of the Luger.

SIG 210 is the general designation of a series of pistols all of which were made primarily to fire either 9 mm or 7.65 mm Parabellum ammunition but which can also be converted to fire .22LR. Conversion from 9 mm to 7.65 mm is effected by a simple change of the barrel and its associated return spring.

General details of the series are given in the entry for the 9 mm version. The 7.65 mm version is not known to be in regular military service; but the series is in widespread use and there may be military, para-military or police applications of this version.

7.65 mm SIG-SAUER P220 AND P230 PISTOLS   (SWITZERLAND/GERMANY)

This entry relates to the versions of the P220 and P230 pistols designed for use with 7.65 mm ammunition.

A fuller description of the P220 family is given in the corresponding 9 mm entry; and apart from the calibre and a very slight difference in weight (about 15 grams) the data in that entry are applicable also the 7.65 mm Parabellum version. The production status, however, is not known at the time of writing.

The P230 family is described in a separate 9 mm entry which covers both 9 mm Police and 9 mm Short (.380ACP) versions. The 7.65 mm Browning version differs little from the latter, except that it has an 8-round magazine, and also entered production late in 1974.

This entry relates to the 7.65 mm (.32ACP) version of the Turkish copy of the German Walther PP pistol. A fuller description of the weapon is given in the corresponding 9 mm entry; and apart from the change of calibre the data given there are equally applicable to the 7.65 mm weapon.

7.65 mm M/908 AND M/915 PISTOLS
(USA)

These pistols are now in military service only in training units of the Portuguese Army. The design is interesting in that it uses a delayed blowback action in which the torque produced by the rifling while the bullet remains in the barrel is used to counter the unlocking motion produced by a lug on the barrel and a twisted slot in the slide. The delay produced appears to have been rather less than desirable. The two models differed only in the design of the cocking piece, the M/915 being rather safer than the M/908.

Ammunition: 7.65 mm (.380ACP)
Operation: Delayed blowback semi-automatic
Magazine: 10-round detachable box
Sights: Blade foresight; notch rear
Rate of fire: 40 rounds/min
Effective range: 40 m
Total length: 16.5 cm (barrel 9.5 cm)
Weight: 0.6 kg
Manufacturer: Savage Arms Corporation
Status: No longer manufactured. See text.

Portuguese M/908 pistol *(RSAF)*.

This is the latest pistol to be made and brought into service in Yugoslavia. Designed to use either the 7.65 mm x 17SR or 9 mm x 17 round, it is a small and light weapon with limited magazine capacity. It is blowback-operated and semi-automatic and incorporates a slide stop and pin similar to that of the 9 mm Browning.

Ammunition: 7.65 mm x 17SR or 9 mm x 17
Operation: Blowback, semi-automatic
Magazine: 6-round detachable box
Sights: Blade foresight; notch rear
Rate of fire: 24 rounds/min
Effective range: 30 m
Total length: 16.5 cm (barrel 9.5 cm)
Weight: 0.8 kg loaded
Manufacturer: Yugoslav State Arsenals
Status: In production and in service with Yugoslav forces.

9 mm STEYR M12 PISTOL   (AUSTRIA)

Although obsolete and long since replaced in Austrian military service by the Walther P38 design built by Steyr-Daimler-Puch, the M12 is mentioned here partly because it may still be encountered and partly because parts of its design have been copied elsewhere — for example in the 0.45 in Mexican Obregon pistol. The particular feature there copied was the rotating-barrel unlocking system in which the barrel is rotated through 60 degrees by threads engaging in recesses in the receiver. Originally designed for the 9 mm Steyr cartridge some were converted during the Second World War to take the 9 mm Parabellum cartridge.

Ammunition: 9 mm Steyr or 9 mm Parabellum
Operation: Short-recoil semi-automatic
Magazine: Fixed; charger-loaded by 8-round clip
Sights: Blade foresight; notch rear
Rate of fire: 24 rounds/min
Effective range: 50 m
Manufacturer: Steyr Waffenfabrik
Status: No longer made. Formerly used by the armed forces of Austria, Chile, Germany (wartime) and in various Balkan countries but now officially obsolete in all of them.

9mm Steyr M12 pistol.

This pistol was manufactured by FN in versions using the 7.65 mm (.32 ACP) cartridge as well as the 9 mm Short (.380 ACP). General details of the weapon will be found in the entry for the 7.65 mm version.

9mm Browning M1910 *(RSAF)*.

9 mm BROWNING HP 35

This was the last pistol to be designed by J.M. Browning and was introduced in 1935. Originally there were two versions, one having fixed sights and the other a tangent rear sight graduated to 500 m and provision for a shoulder stock. The pistol was first produced in Belgium but was subsequently made in Canada during the German occupation of Belgium; and pistols from the latter source were used extensively by British, Canadian and Chinese forces in the Second World War.

Still in widespread use in the simpler version the pistol is known as the GP (Grande Puissance) in Belgium and the Netherlands, as the FN 9 mm HP No 1 Mks 1 and 1* in Canada, as the M/46 in Denmark and the 640(b) in West Germany and as the FN Browning No 2 Mk 1 in the UK.

9mm Browning HP pistol with fixed rearsight.

DATA (Current Belgian production)
Ammunition: 9 mm parabellum
Operation: Recoil-operated semi-automatic
Magazine: 13-round detachable box
Sights: Barleycorn foresight; U-notch rear
Rate of fire: Single shot, 40 rounds/min
Effective range: 45 m
Total length: 20 cm (barrel 11 cm)
Weight: 0.9 kg empty; 1.1 kg loaded
Date introduced: 1935
Manufacturer: FN (Belgium) and others (see text)
Status: In service (in Belgian and Canadian versions) in Australia, Belgium, Canada, Denmark, Indonesia, Netherlands, Taiwan and UK.

Canadian production of the FN HP pistol was by John Inglis who produced a total of five versions of the weapon. Of these only the No 2 Mark 1* is officially in service with Canadian forces (and is used by Australian and British forces) but earlier models still exist. The full range comprises the following variants

No 1 Mark 1	Tangent leaf rear sight graduated 60-500 m with provision for shoulder stock and holster
No 1 Mark 1*	Similar to the Mk 1 but with a modified ejector and extractor
No 2 Mark 1	As No 1 Mk 1 but with a fixed U-notch rear sight and no provision for a shoulder stock
No 2 Mark 1*	As No 2 Mk 1 but with the modified ejector and extractor
Lightweight Model	As No 2 Mk 1* but with grooves cut in the slide to reduce weight.

Status: As noted above. Spare parts are made by Long Branch Arsenal at Ontario.

Canadian-made HP No 1 Mark 1 with Chinese markings *(RSAF)*.

Canadian-made HP No 2 Mark 1* pistol *(RSAF)*.

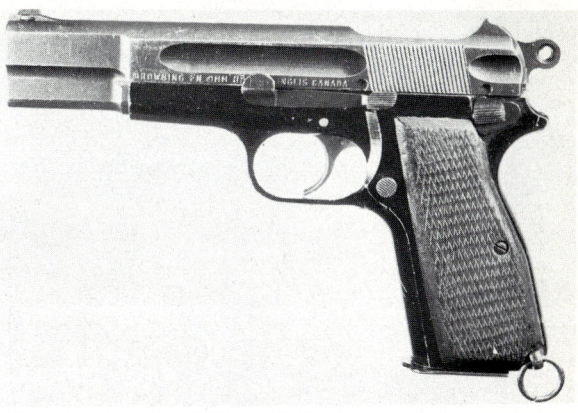

Lightened version of the No 2 Mark 1* *(RSAF)*.

This is the designation by which the Chinese copy of the Russian 9 mm Makarov SL pistol is known. The pistols are marked '59 SH1' on the receiver, otherwise details are the same as those given in the Russian entry.

Manufacturer: State factories
Status: In service.

9 mm Vz 38 AND Vz 38/39 PISTOLS

This blowback-operated weapon is similar in function to the 7.62 mm Vz 27 but has a modified trigger mechanism which will function only at double action but can be thumbset at half cock. The barrel is secured by a collar pinned to the front of the receiver: with the slide removed it can be tilted from the rear for examination or cleaning.

Because the Vz 38 was unsatisfactory in several respects an improved version, known as the Vz 38/39 was produced.

Ammunition: 9 mm Short (.380ACP)
Operation: Blowback, semi-automatic
Magazine: 8-round detachable box
Sights: Blade foresight; notch rear
Rate of fire: 30 rounds/min
Effective range: 40 m
Total length: 20 cm (barrel 12 cm)
Weight: 0.9 kg
Manufacturer: Ceskoslovenska Zbrojovka
Status: Obsolescent and no longer in production.

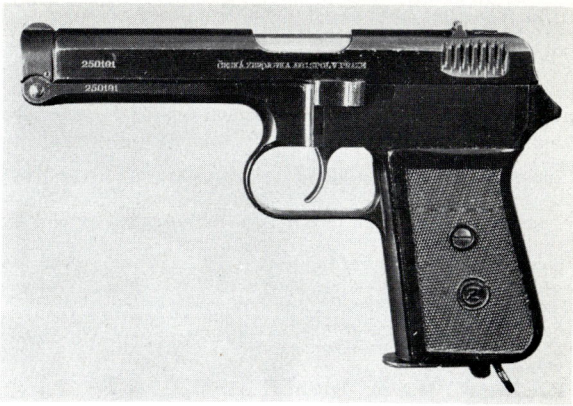

9mm Vz 38/39 pistol *(RSAF)*.

(FINLAND)

This pistol has been in service since it replaced the 9 mm Luger as the standard weapon of the Finnish Army in 1935. In appearance it resembles the Luger and it strips similarly but the action is different and incorporates features from Bergmann-Bayard and Browning designs. A unique feature is the inclusion of an accelerator which speeds the rearward motion of the breech-block when the barrel is brought to rest.

Well-sealed against dirt and moisture the Lahti M 35 is well-known for its reliability; and this presumably accounts for the long service life of a relatively heavy weapon.

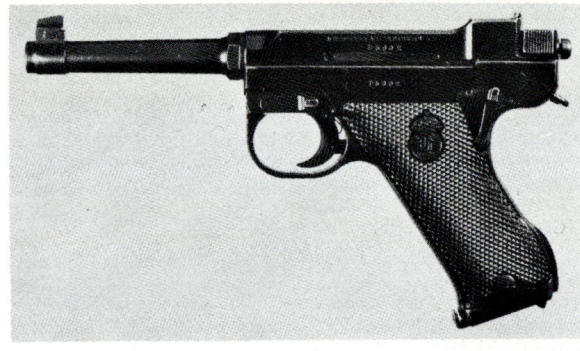

Lahti 9mm M35 pistol *(RSAF)*.

Ammunition: 9 mm Parabellum
Operation: Short-recoil, semi-automattic
Magazine: 8-round detachable box
Sights: Blade foresight; notch rear
Rate of fire: 30 rounds/min
Effective range: 40 m
Total length: 24.5 cm (barrel 10.5 cm)
Weight: 1.2 kg
Date introduced: 1935
Manufacturer: VKT
Status: In service in Finland and in slightly modified form in Sweden.

9 mm MAS MODEL 1950 PISTOL

Generally similar in design to the Colt 1911A1, this pistol has for many years been the standard French Army weapon. It was designed at the arsenal at St. Etienne.

An important difference between this weapon and the Colt is the slide-mounted safety arrangement. Pulling back the rear end of the slide and then releasing it positions the cartridge in the chamber and an indicator to the rear of the ejection slot indicates that the chamber is loaded. The safety-catch is on the left rear of the slide and is at safe when its lever is horizontal. In this condition the hammer can be lowered safely by pulling the trigger because the safety device prevents the hammer from striking the firing pin.

Ammunition: 9 mm Parabellum
Operation: Recoil, self-loading single-action
Magazine: 9-round detachable box
Sights: Blade foresight; notch rear
Rate of fire: 30 rounds/min
Effective range: 50 m
Total length: 19.5 cm (barrel 11 cm)
Weight: 0.9 kg
Manufacturer: Chatellerault and St. Etienne arsenals
Status: In service in the French Army and elsewhere but no longer in production.

9mm MAS Model 1950.

This is one of a range of pistols produced by MAB for commercial and military use and is the one adopted by the French Army. Mechanically, it is unusual in employing the delayed blowback operating principle: the barrel is prevented from recoiling relative to the receiver and initially locks the slide also; but rotation of a barrel lug in a cam slot, under the initial gas pressure, releases the slide to complete the mechanical cycle when the pressure is at a safe level.

Ammunition: 9 mm Parabellum
Operation: Delayed blowback semi-automatic
Magazine: 15-round detachable box
Sights: Blade foresight; notch rear
Rate of fire: 40 rounds/min
Effective range: 50 m
Total length: 20.5 cm (barrel 11.5 cm)
Weight: 1.1 kg
Manufacturer: MAB
Status: In production and in French Army service.

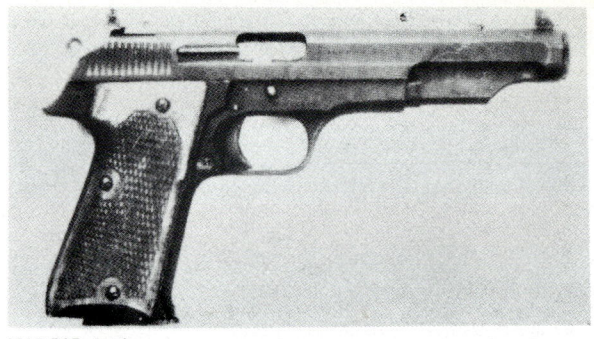

MAB P15 pistol.

9 mm MAB P8 PISTOL

This is a slightly smaller member of the MAB series. It has an 8-round magazine and a correspondingly smaller grip but is otherwise similar to the P15.

9 mm MAUSER 1896 PISTOL

Against a German government contract placed in 1916 a substantial quantity of Mauser pistols of the 1896 pattern was produced to fire the 9 mm Parabellum instead of the 7.63 mm Mauser round. To distinguish them from the smaller-calibre weapons, many of these pistols were marked with a large figure 9 on the grip — usually in red. Examples of these pistols may still be encountered.

An earlier 9 mm weapon was the Mauser Export which was chambered for the straight-sided Mauser Export cartridge. This was a more powerful round than the Parabellum, with a muzzle velocity some 20% higher, but only a few pistols of this type were manufactured. Some were supplied to the Persian government.

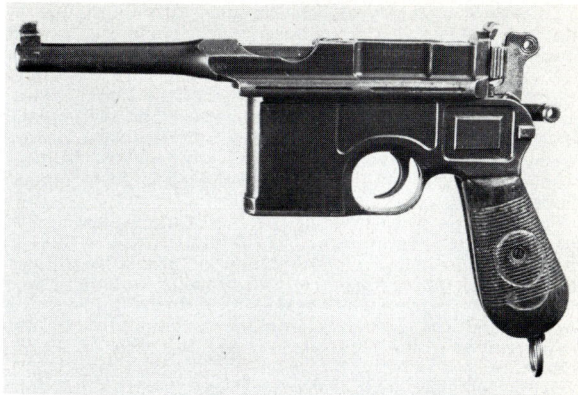

Mauser pistol converted to 9mm calibre *(RSAF)*.

This famous pistol was first accepted for military use (by the Swiss) in 1900 and has been in service, in one form or another, ever since then. The earliest models, and some of the later variants, were chambered for the 7.65 mm Luger round; but it is as a 9 mm weapon that the Luger is best known. Although very many different versions of the pistol have been produced the departures from the basic design have never been very great and the current Mauser production is very similar in appearance to the DWM version made in 1900.

Probably the most familiar feature of the weapon is its toggle-joint locking system. The function of this is to keep the breech locked while the chamber pressure is high, during which period the barrel, bolt and joint assembly recoil for a short distance and at the end of which the toggle lock is broken and the breech opens. A consequence of this arrangement is that the weapon will fire only as a self-loader.

Typical data are given below for a version with a four-inch (103 mm) barrel. Very large numbers of these short-barrelled Lugers were made for military use between 1938 and 1943: another familiar version was the "artillery" weapon with an eight inch barrel and a tangent leaf backsight. Versions in 7.65 mm calibre are separately described.

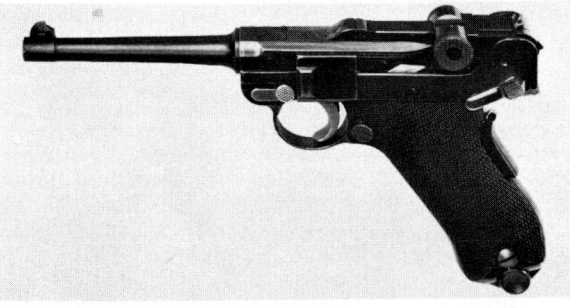

Model 1906 Luger *(RMCS)*.

Ammunition: 9 mm Parabellum
Operation: Short recoil, single-action, self-loading
Magazine: 8-round box. (A 32-round snail magazine was used with some long-barrelled versions.)
Sights: Blade foresight; notch rear. (Tangent rear sight on some long-barrelled weapons.)
Rate of fire: 32 rounds/min
Effective range: 50 m. (Maximum range capability with long barrel about 1,400 m)

9mm Luger Artillery model with 8-inch barrel and 32-round snail magazine *(RSAF)*.

Total length: 22 cm (barrel 10.5 cm)
Weight: 0.9 kg
Manufacturer: Many in Germany: also made in Switzerland by Waffenfabrik, Bern, and briefly by Vickers in England. Current commercial manufacture by Mauser.
Status: Some two million of all versions have been made in more than 75 years. Although not known to be official issue to any regular formation, therefore, there are certainly still a great many Lugers about.

(GERMANY — BRD)

This is the current version of the Walther P38 which was used by the German Army in the Second World War. Apart from the markings the main differences between the P38 and the P1 are the light dural receiver and improved firing pin design of the latter. Both weapons feature short-recoil operation and a choice of single or double-action firing, it being possible to cock the hammer manually for single-action operation. If the safety is operated when the weapon is thus cocked the hammer will go forward to the uncocked position but the spindle of the safety lever locks the firing pin so that it cannot be driven foward by the hammer.

Ammunition: 9 mm Parabellum
Operation: Short recoil, self-loading, double-action
Magazine: 8-round detachable box
Sights: Blade foresight; U-notch rear
Rate of fire: 32 rounds/min
Effective range: 50 m
Total length: 22 cm (barrel 12.5 cm)
Weight: 0.9 kg
Date introduced: P38 in 1938; P1 in 1957
Manufacturer: Walther
Status: More than a million P38 weapons were made between 1938 and the end of the war and the P1 has been in production since 1957. The weapons are in service in W. Germany and in many other countries including Chile, Norway and Sweden.

9mm Model P1 pistol *(RSAF)*.

9 mm WALTHER PP AND PPK PISTOLS

Of the four calibres in which the Walther PP and PPK pistols have been produced, 7.65 mm and 9 mm are the two most important. Details of the weapons are given in the entry in the 7.65 mm calibre division of this section: it is sufficient to note here that in addition to the Walther manufacture, the 9 mm version has been produced by Manurhin (PPK version) in France and by MKE (PP version) in Turkey. There are small differences of detail between the German versions and the others. The Russian 9 mm Makarov pistol is also based on the PP but differs from it more significantly.

These two pistols differ only in that the P9 has a single-action and the P9S a double-action trigger. Both are operated by delayed blowback using a system derived from the action of the G3 rifle made by the same manufacturers. The delay is achieved by the use of locking rollers which must be driven down angled faces to the unlocked position before the bolt can make its major rearward excursion. The resistance presented jointly by the angled faces and the return spring results in a very small initial bolt movement while the chamber pressure is high.

The pistols have loaded-chamber indicators which can be detected by touch and have polygonal rifling to ease maintenance and improve accuracy. There is a choice of barrel lengths.

Heckler and Koch Model P9.

Ammunition: 9 mm x 19 Parabellum
Operation: Delayed blowback, self-loading, single-action (P9) or double-action (P9S)
Magazine: 9-round detachable box
Sights: Blade foresight; notch rear. A click sight can be fitted
Total length: 13.5 cm or 15 cm (barrel 10 cm or 11.5 cm)
Weight: 1.1 kg loaded
Manufacturer: Heckler and Koch
Status: Production. Sold commercially and used by German police. Suitable for military use but not known to have been so used.

Heckler and Koch Model P9S with modified trigger guard.

9 mm HECKLER AND KOCH VP70 AUTOMATIC PISTOL

This blowback-operated weapon can be used either as a hand-held self-loading pistol firing single rounds or, fitted with a shoulder stock, as an automatic weapon firing three-round bursts at a cyclic rate of 2,200 rounds/min. The design has few moving parts and makes considerable use of plastics. A life of 30,000 rounds is claimed by the manufacturers.

The simple blowback action is controlled solely by the return spring, a new round being chambered on the return stroke: if the magazine is empty the slide must be withdrawn and released to chamber a round when the full magazine is inserted. A loaded chamber is indicated by the extractor position. The firing pin is not cocked when the round is chambered but is cocked when the first trigger pressure is taken and released on the second pressure.

For the SMG conversion the pistol is attached to a holster stock which can also be used as a convenient transit case. The holster carries the selector lever which can be set to single shots or three-round bursts. To accommodate a reasonable number of bursts, the pistol has an 18-round magazine.

Heckler and Koch VP70.

Ammunition: 9 mm x 19 Parabellum
Operation: Blowback single-shot or burst fire
Magazine: 18-round box
Sights: Blade foresight; notch rear
Rate of fire: 40 rounds/min self-loading or 100 rounds/min in 3-round bursts with 2,200 rounds/min cyclic rate
Effective range: 50 m hand-held; 150 m when fired from shoulder
Total length: Pistol 20.5 cm; pistol with stock 54.5 cm; barrel 11.5 cm
Weight: Pistol unloaded: 0.8 kg; pistol loaded: 1.1 kg; pistol plus stock loaded: 1.6 kg
Manufacturer: Heckler and Koch
Status: Production. No known military sales.

VP70 with holster stock attached.

(GERMANY — BRD)

Although it has not so far been adopted by any regular military formation this weapon is used extensively by police forces and is currently in production for commercial sale. It has been made in 7.65 mm, 6.35 mm and .22LR calibres as well as in 9 mm and a feature of the design is the ease with which models can be converted from one calibre to another and from centre-fire to rimfire. Simple blowback is the operating principle and the weapon has a double-action trigger mechanism. Calibre change is by simple exchange of barrels and magazines: change from centre-fire to rimfire involves adjusting the breech face plate.

Ammunition: 9 mm (.380ACP)
Operation: Blowback with double-action firing
Magazine: 8-round detachable box
Sights: Blade foresight; notch rear
Rate of fire: 30 rounds/min
Effective range: 25-30 m
Total length: 15.5 cm (barrel 8.5 cm)
Weight: 0.6 kg
Manufacturer: Heckler and Koch
Status: Production. In police service but not known to be in military service.

Heckler and Koch HK4 pistol.

9 mm PISTOLE M

This East German Army weapon is a copy of the Russian Makarov pistol, which in turn is copied from the Walther PP. It is an eight-shot, blowback-operated, self-loading pistol which fires the 9 mm x 18 cartridge developed for it. It can be fired either with double-action trigger operation or, by manual cocking, with single-action operation. External differences from the Walther PP are the absence of a loaded-chamber indicator, an externally operated slide stop (that on the Walther is totally enclosed) and a safety-catch which goes up instead of down for 'safe'.

Ammunition: 9 mm x 18
Operation: Blowback, self-loading
Magazine: 8-round detachable box
Sights: Blade foresight; notch rear
Rate of fire: 35 rounds/min
Effective range: 50 m
Total length: 16 cm (barrel 9 cm)
Weight: 0.7 kg
Manufacturer: DDR State factories
Status: In service in the East Germany Army.

Pistole M *(RSAF)*.

9 mm M1937 PISTOL

This is a 9 mm Short (.380ACP) version of the standard 7.65 mm M1937 pistol, the entry for which should be consulted for further details. The 9 mm weapon is now probably rare.

9 mm WALAM 48 PISTOL

This is a copy of the German Walther PP made in the 9 mm Short (.380ACP) calibre. It was made for sale to Egypt but the few produced were sold commercially. A 7.65 mm version was made in larger quantities and is described separately.

9 mm PA-63 PISTOL

Based on the German Walther PP pistol, this is a light 9 mm weapon and is the latest of several such pistols to be produced for Hungarian military use. It is a double-action blowback-operated weapon similar in appearance to the PP but somewhat less bulky.

Calibre: 9 mm
Operation: Blowback-operated double-action
Magazine: 7-round detachable box
Sights: Blade foresight; notch rear
Effective range: 50 m
Total length: 17.5 cm (barrel 8.5 cm)
Weight: 0.7 kg
Manufacturer: State factories
Status: In limited service in the Hungarian Army.

9 mm TOKAGYPT PISTOL

(HUNGARY)

This Hungarian version of the Russian Tokarev TT-33 pistol was produced in 9 mm calibre (9 mm x 19 Parabellum) for sale to Egypt and for use by the Egyptian Army. So far as is known, however, it was never used by that army: a few were diverted to police forces but the bulk appear to have been put on commercial sale.

Apart from the calibre the Tokagypt differs from the TT-33 in having a safety catch on the receiver, a plastic grip round the handle and a finger spur on the floor plate of the magazine. Other data will be found in the TT-33 entry.

This weapon has never been in service with Hungarian forces; but a 7.62 mm version, known as the Model 48, is a standard Hungarian Army weapon and is separately described.

The Tokagypt.

(INDONESIA)

9 mm PINDAD PISTOL

Made by the Ordnance Factory at Pindad this pistol is a licence-built copy of the FN Browning HP pistol. The principal difference between the Indonesian and Belgian weapons is the absence of a version of the former with a tangent leaf backsight. The Pindad is marked "Fabrik Sendjata Ringan" and, below, "Pindad P1A9 mm".

Ammunition: 9 mm x 19 Parabellum
Operation: Recoil-operated semi-automatic
Magazine: 13-round detachable box
Sights: Blade foresight; notch rear
Rate of fire: 39 rounds/min
Effective range: 50 m
Total length: 20 cm (barrel 11 cm)
Weight: 0.9 kg
Manufacturer: Pindad Ordnance Factory
Status: In service with Indonesian forces.

9mm Pindad pistol.

9 mm BERETTA MODEL 1934 PISTOL

(ITALY)

This pistol was preceded by models of 1915, 1921 and 1923 and is an improved version incorporating the best features of its predecessors and designed primarily for the 9 mm Short (.380ACP) cartridge. It is a blowback-operated weapon incorporating a disconnector mechanism in the trigger chain to leave the hammer cocked when the slide moves forward to chamber a round. The safety catch operates on the trigger and there is no lock on the hammer.

A version in 7.65 mm is known as the Model 1935 and is described separately.

Ammunition: 9 mm Short (.380ACP). See text
Operation: Blowback, semi-automatic
Magazine: 7-round detachable box
Sights: Blade foresight; notch rear
Rate of fire: 28 rounds/min
Effective range: 40 m
Total length: 15 cm (barrel 9 cm)
Weight: 0.6 kg
Date introduced: 1934
Manufacturer: Beretta
Status: In production and in Italian Army service.

9mm Beretta M1934.

(ITALY)

This is the standard Italian Army weapon and is used also in Egypt, Israel and Nigeria. It has a short recoil action with a swinging-arm locking system similar to that of the German Walther P38 and P1 pistols. As the barrel, breech and slide recoil together an unlocking plunger on the rear barrel lug is arrested by the receiver; and as the slide and barrel continue rearwards the plunger forces the barrel locking piece down into recesses in the slide, thus allowing the slide and breech block to complete the extraction cocking and reloading cycle while the barrel is brought to rest. A single-action trigger mechanism is used: in the event of a misfire the hammer is recocked by hand.

Ammunition: 9 mm x 19 Parabellum
Operation: Short-recoil, self-loading, single-action
Magazine: 8-round detachable box
Sights: Blade foresight; notch rear
Rate of fire: 32 rounds/min
Effective range: 50 m
Total length: 20.5 cm (barrel 11.5 cm)
Weight: 0.9 kg with steel receiver; 0.8 kg with dural receiver
Date introduced: 1951
Manufacturer: Beretta
Status: In production and service (see text).

9mm Beretta M1951

9 mm NEW NAMBU MODEL 57A AUTOMATIC PISTOL (JAPAN)

This is a self-loading pistol, the word 'automatic' in the title being the manufacturer's designation. Although designed for military use and in limited production it is believed not to have been adopted yet by the Japanese forces. The design is similar to that of the American Colt M1911A1 which is currently the standard Japanese Army pistol.

Ammunition: 9 mm x 19 Parabellum
Operation: Recoil-operated self-loading
Magazine: 8-round detachable box
Sights: Blade foresight; notch rear
Rate of fire: 24 rounds/min
Effective range: 50 m
Total length: 20 cm (barrel 12 cm)
Weight: 0.9 kg
Manufacturer: Shin Chuo Kogyo Co
Status: Limited production.

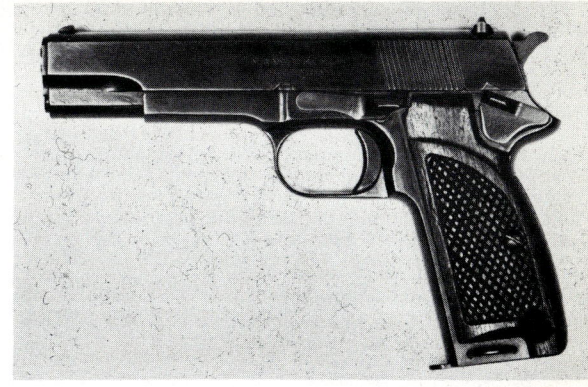

New Nambu Model 57A.

This pistol is also sometimes known as the VIS from the initials (of the designers) on the grip. Incorporating some of the design features of the Colt M1911A1 and the FN HP pistols it was the standard Polish military pistol from 1935 until the German occupation; after which it was made for German use in a less well-finished model — known as the 35(S) — with German markings in place of the Polish eagle. It has a short-recoil mechanism using the Browning pattern of shaped lug on the underside of the recoiling barrel to disengage it from the slide. When cocked and with a round in the chamber the hammer can be safely lowered by a thumb catch on the slide. The magazine holding-open device is of the Colt type.

9mm Radom pistol *(RMCS)*.

Ammunition: 9 mm Parabellum
Operation: Short-recoil semi-automatic
Magazine: 8-round detachable box
Sights: Blade foresight; notch rear
Rate of fire: 32 rounds/min
Effective range: 50 m
Total length: 19.5 cm (barrel 12 cm)
Weight: 1.0 kg
Date introduced: 1935
Manufacturer: Fabryka Broni Radom
Status: No longer made. In service in Poland at least.

9 mm P-64 SL PISTOL

(POLAND)

This pistol was introduced into Polish military service to replace the 7.62 mm Pistolet TT which was identical to the Russian TT-33 except for the grips. The P-64 is similar in appearance to the Russian 9 mm Makarov but is a Polish design which incorporates some features of the German Walther PP. Initially or after applying the safety, which lowers the hammer without operating the firing pin, the pistol is fired by double-action trigger operation or it can be hand-cocked for single-action: at other times cocking is automatic by blowback and the trigger action single.

Ammunition: 9 mm x 18
Operation: Blowback self-loading with single or double-action firing
Magazine: 6-round detachable box
Sights: Blade foresight; notch rear
Rate of fire: 30 rounds/min
Effective range: 50 m
Total length: 15.5 cm (barrel 8.5 cm)
Weight: 0.6 kg
Date introduced: 1964
Manufacturer: State factories
Status: In production and in service with Polish forces.

Russian Makarov (top) and Polish P64 pistols.

Of a wide variety of pistols made by the various Spanish companies whose titles are generally grouped under the name Astra, those most likely to be encountered in military or para-military use today are the Model 400 (the 'water-pistol') and its derivatives, the Model 300 (.32ACP but mainly .380ACP) and Model 600 (9 mm Parabellum), both of which were supplied to the German Army.

The Model 400 entered production in 1921 and was adopted as the standard weapon for the Spanish Army. It was designed primarily to use the 9 mm Largo round but was supposed to be able to accept smaller 9 mm rounds. This appears not to have been a satisfactory arrangement, however, and was probably the reason why the German Army specified a 9 mm Parabellum version for the otherwise similar Model 600. The Model 300 was smaller and lighter.

Although the Model 400 was first conceived as a delayed-blowback weapon, the majority were produced as simple blowback devices using heavy recoil and hammer springs to cope with the powerful cartridge. It had an 8-round magazine which was fitted with grip, slide and magazine safety devices and weighed about 1 kg. The pistol was 20.5 cm long and had a 13.5 cm barrel.

The Model 300 derivative was shorter (16.5 cm with a 9 cm barrel) and lighter and in the .380ACP version (which was made in the larger quantity) the magazine holds only six rounds. The other version held seven.

None of these pistols is in official military service today.

9 mm SUPER STAR PISTOL

Although this pistol is similar in appearance to the Colt M1911A1 it uses the FN Browning type of barrel locking cam; also the trigger pivots instead of sliding and there is no grip safety. The weapon in its 9 mm Largo version is the standard Spanish Army pistol: it is also made commercially in other calibres (9 mm Parabellum, 0.45 in ACP and 0.38 in Super Auto)

Ammunition: 9 mm Largo
Operation: Short recoil semi-automatic
Magazine: 9-round detachable box
Sights: Blade foresight; V-notch rear
Rate of fire: 36 rounds/min
Effective range: 50 m
Total length: 20.5 cm (barrel 13.5 cm)
Weight: 1.0 kg
Manufacturer: Bonifacio Echeverria
Status: In service with Spanish forces.

9mm Super Star pistol *(RSAF)*.

SIG 210 is the designation of a family of military, police and target pistols which are made mainly in 9 mm and 7.65 mm calibres. The SIG 210-2 which is also known by the official designation Model 49 is the current Swiss military pistol and differs from the SIG 210-1 only in the finish of the grips, the former being sand-blasted to give a non-reflecting surface. The pistols use a Colt-Browning type of short recoil action, but the slide is carried inside the frame, instead of wrapping round the outside, and a slide stop is fitted. Conversion between 9 mm and 7.65 mm calibre is by simple exchange of barrels and return springs: conversion to .22LR is also possible by changing the barrel, spring, slide and magazine. The 210-5 (15 cm barrel) and 210-6 (12 cm barrel) are target pistols with adjustable sights. All versions are very well made and the target pistols are widely used in competitions.

SIG P210 pistol.

DATA (210-1 and 210-2 only)
Ammunition: 9 mm Parabellum (see text)
Operation: Short recoil self-loading
Magazine: 8-round detachable box magazine
Sights: Blade foresight; notch rear
Rate of fire: 32 rounds/min
Effective range: 50 m
Total length: 21.5 cm (barrel 12 cm)
Weight: 1.0 kg
Date introduced: 1949 in Swiss Army
Manufacturer: SIG
Status: In commercial production. In Swiss and Danish military service and police service elsewhere. To be replaced in the Swiss Army by the Model 75.

Swiss military Model 49.

9 mm SIG MODEL 75 PISTOL

An order for 10,000 P220 pistols has been placed with SIG for the Swiss Army. The pistol has been given the military designation M75 and it will replace the M49 pistol currently in service.

(SWITZERLAND/GERMANY)

9 mm SIG-SAUER P220 PISTOL

This designation relates to a family of pistols with a common design and a choice of four calibres. The basis is a double-action short-recoil weapon which can be hand cocked to fire with a single-action pull. After the short recoil the barrel is unlocked from the slide by a ramp which tilts it down and halts it against a stop. There is no applied safety for the weapon but it is maintained in a safe condition by a pin which locks the firing pin and is disengaged only when the trigger is pulled.

Ammunition: 9 mm Parabellum; also designed for 0.38 Super, .45ACP and 7.65 mm Parabellum
Operation: Short recoil, self-loading double-action
Magazine: 9-round detachable box
Sights: Von Stavenhagen contrast sights. Blade foresight with square notch rearsight
Rate of fire: 40 rounds/min
Effective range: 50 m
Total length: 20 cm (barrel 11 cm)
Weight: 0.8 kg
Manufacturer: Sauer (Joint project initiated by SIG)
Status: Production. Designed for use as a military pistol and produced in Germany because of Swiss restrictions on arms exports. Production status of .38 Super version, which has characteristics generally similar to those listed above, is not known. The .45 and 7.65 mm versions have separate entries. See also the entry for the Model 75.

9mm P220 pistol.

9 mm SIG-SAUER P230 PISTOL

This pistol has been designed with the police and para-military markets primarily in mind but may also find military applications. A new cartridge, intermediate between the military 9 mm Parabellum and the 9 mm Short (.380ACP) and called the 9 mm Police, has been developed for use with one version of the pistol: another version, with a lighter slide, will fire the 9 mm Short. A further version for use with 7.65 mm Browning ammunition has also been made and a .22LR conversion kit will be available.

The P230 is similar in many respects to the P220 including the hammer and trigger action. The main operating principle, however, is blowback.

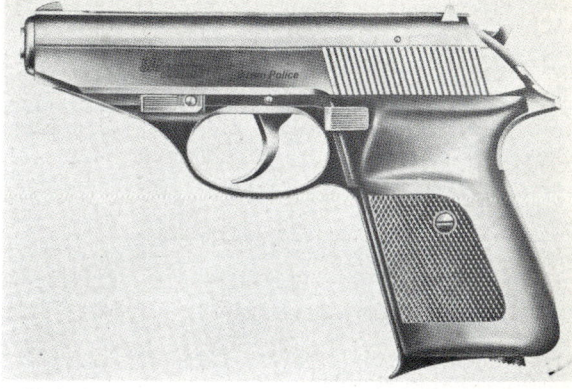

P230 pistol.

Ammunition: 9 mm Police or 9 mm Short (.380ACP). Also made for 7.65 mm Browning and convertible to .22Lr
Operation: Blowback, single or double-action
Magazine: 7-round detachable box
Sights: Von Stavenhagen contrast sights; blade and notch
Rate of fire: 40 rounds/min
Effective range: 40 m or 30 m (9 mm Short)
Total length: 17 cm (barrel 9 cm)
Weight: 0.7 kg or 0.5 kg (9 mm Short)
Manufacturer: Sauer
Status: Production. See P220 entry for SIG-Sauer arrangement.

(SWEDEN)

This a Swedish-made copy of the Finnish Lahti pistol. Like the Lahti, it is an improvement on the Luger design, the toggle-joint having been replaced by a fully-enclosed locking block which slides in slots in the receiver and breech block. It also employs a Browning-type accelerator to maximise the recoil energy in the breech block and uses a conventional sear and internal hammer in place of the side-operating sear of the Luger.

Ammunition: 9 mm Parabellum
Operation: Short recoil
Magazine: 8-round detachable box
Sights: Blade foresight; notch rear
Rate of fire: 32 rounds/min
Effective range: 50 m
Total length: 27 cm (barrel 14 cm)
Weight: 1.1 kg
Date introduced: 1940
Manufacturer: Husqvarna
Status: No longer in production. In Swedish Army service.

9mm Husqvarna Model 40.

9 mm MKE PISTOL

This pistol is similar in design to the German Walther PP: it has the same mechanism and differs externally only in minor details such as the shape of the magazine finger rest.

Ammunition: 9 mm Short (.380ACP); also made in 7.65 mm (.32ACP)
Operation: Blowback
Magazine: 7-round detachable box
Sights: Blade foresight; notch rear
Rate of fire: 35 rounds/min
Effective range: 30 m
Total length: 17 cm (barrel 10 cm)
Weight: 0.7 kg
Manufacturer: MKE
Status: In production and in service with the Turkish Army.

9mm MKE pistol.

This is a true automatic pistol capable of continuous fire, while the ammunition lasts, when held in the hand or used with a shoulder stock. Like all other automatic weapons it has the disadvantage that the muzzle tends to rise, when automatic fire is selected, because of the turning moment of the recoil force about the mean point of support. Aim is more easily controlled if the holster shoulder stock is used.

The Stechkin is blowback operated and has a fairly conventional closed breech single or double-action operation when single shots are selected. At full automatic, however, the semi-automatic process is short-circuited. As the slide moves to the rear, energy is extracted from it by a retarder device, thus slowing the slide down; and this energy is used, when the slide cycle is complete, to fire the weapon. The pistol is fitted with an applied safety and an empty-magazine holding-open device.

9mm Stechkin pistol.

Ammunition: 9 mm x 18
Operation: Blowback; selective fire; double action
Magazine: 20-round detachable box
Sights: Blade foresight; notch rear
Rate of fire: 40 rounds/min (semi-automatic); 80 rounds/min (automatic); 750 rounds/min cyclic
Effective range: 50 m, or 200 m with stock attached
Total length: Pistol, 22.5 cm; pistol and stock 54 cm; barrel 12.5 cm
Weight: Pistol empty: 1.0 kg; pistol, empty, with stock: 1.6 kg; pistol and stock loaded: 1.8 kg
Manufacturer: State factories
Status: No longer produced or in first-line Russian service. Still in service with border guards and may be used elsewhere.

Stechkin with holster stock attached.

This pistol is in widespread use, in various versions, throughout Eastern Europe and in many Asian and other client countries of Russia or China. It is made in East Germany as the Pistole M and in China as the Type 59. Based on the German Walther PP pistol it differs from it mainly in having a spring magazine catch, and an externally-mounted slide stop and in lacking a loaded-chamber indicator. It is a blowback-operated weapon relying on the low-powered round and the inertia and resistance of the slide and return spring to prevent premature opening of the breech. The slide stop can be used to close the breech on an empty magazine: otherwise a round is automatically chambered when a new magazine is inserted.

9mm Makarov pistol.

Ammunition: 9 mm x 18
Operation: Blowback; self-loading; double-action
Magazine: 8-round detachable box
Sights: Blade foresight; notch rear
Rate of fire: 35 rounds min
Effective range: 50 m
Total length: 16 cm (barrel 9 cm)
Weight: 0.7 kg
Manufacturer: State factories
Status: In production and service (see text).

9 mm COLT MODEL 1971 MILITARY PISTOL

This is a modern double-action 9 mm pistol which has been designed to retain many of the handling characteristics of the M1911. Apart from the change from 0.45 in to 9 mm calibre new features include the extensive use of stainless steel alloys, a 15-shot magazine and a double-action trigger which, combined with a safety acting directly on the firing pin, makes it possible to carry the pistol safely with a round in the chamber.

Ammunition: 9 mm Parabellum
Operation: Short recoil; double-action
Magazine: 15-round detachable box
Sights: Blade foresight;notch rear
Rate of fire: 35 rounds/min
Effective range: 50 m
Total length: 20 cm (barrel 11.5 cm)
Weight: 1.0 kg
Manufacturer: Colt
Status: Production.

9 mm COLT COMBAT COMMANDER PISTOL

This is one of three versions of a M1911A1 derivative introduced by Colt in 1971. Fuller details are given in the corresponding 0.45 in entry. The third version is chambered for the .38 in Super round.

These two pistols are commercially-produced weapons of a type that may be found in military or para-military service. Both are designed to take the 9 mm Parabellum round and both have micrometer rear sights and four inch (102 mm) barrels. Empty weight is approximately 0.8 kg: the No 39 has an 8-round and the No 59 a 14-round magazine.

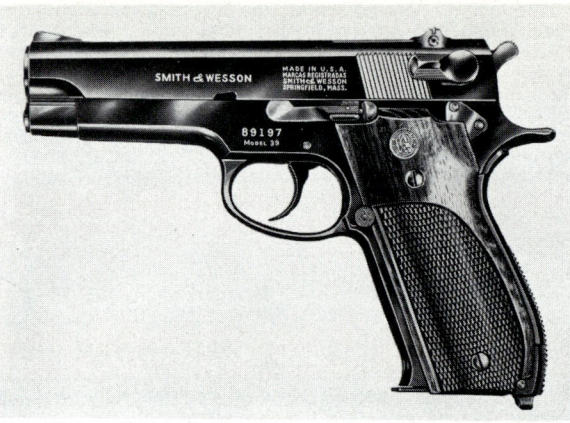

Smith & Wesson Model 59.

Smith & Wesson Model 39 double-action pistol.

9 mm M65 PISTOL

This is a version of the Yugoslav 7.62 mm M57 pistol — itself a copy of the Russian Tokarev TT-33 — built to accept the 9 mm x 19 Parabellum round. No other differences between the 9 mm and 7.62 mm versions are known. The M65 is both manufactured and in service in Yugoslavia.

9 mm M67 PISTOL

This version of the most recent Yugoslav pistol is designed to take the 9 mm x 17 round. Available details of the weapon will be found in the corresponding entry for the 7.65 mm version.

0.45 in BALLESTER MOLINA M1927 PISTOL

This is a simplified version of the Colt M1911A1 pistol which was manufactured in considerable numbers by HAFDASA, Buenos Aires, and was widely used during the Second World War, notably by undercover groups, among whom it enjoyed a high reputation for functioning under adverse conditions. The magazine is interchangeable with that of the Colt and the differences beween the two weapons are minor: the trigger pivots instead of sliding, there is a trigger extension on the right of the grip to operate the disconnector and the hammer strut is smaller.

Ammunition: .45 Colt ACP
Operation: Recoil
Magazine: 7-round detachable box
Sights: Blade foresight; U-notch rear
Rate of fire: 35 rounds/min
Effective range: 50 m
Total length: 21.5 cm (barrel 12.5 cm)
Weight: 1 kg
Date introduced: 1927
Manufacturer: HAFDASA
Status: Still in service but obsolescent and no longer in production.

Ballester Molina pistol *(RSAF)*.

COLT MODELS 1916 AND 1927 AND SYSTEMS COLT

Prior to the introduction of the Ballester Molina, Colt Models 1911 and 1911A1 were purchased, marked with Argentinian markings and serial numbers and taken into service as Models 1916 and 1927 respectively. A licence-built copy of the 1911A1 (Systems Colt) was also made in the ordnance factory at Rosario and is still in service.

0.45 in OBREGON PISTOL

(MEXICO)

This is the only pistol to have been made in Mexico; and although it is no longer manufactured and has been replaced in first-line service by the Colt M1911A1 it continues in service with second-line units. Its short recoil operating system uses a locking mechanism similar to that of the Austrian Steyr Model 12: a helical lug on the underside of the barrel engages with a stationary cam slot, as the barrel recoils, and rotates the barrel to disengage it from the slide. On the return movement a disconnector operates to isolate the trigger from the sear until the slide is fully forward.

0.45 in Obregon pistol *(J. E. Smith).*

Ammunition: 0.45ACP
Operation: Short recoil semi-automatic
Magazine: 7-round detachable box
Sights: Blade foresight; notch rear
Rate of fire: 32 rounds/min
Effective range: 50 m
Total length: 21.5 cm (barrel 12.5 cm)
Weight: 1.1 kg
Manufacturer: Fabrica de Armas
Status: No longer in production. Still in service (see text).

These designations apply to the Norwegian licence-built copies of the Colt M1911A1. Together with quantities of the same model purchased from the USA both before the First World War and after the Second World War, these pistols have been a standard service issue to the Norwegian forces for sixty years or more. The M1912 is a direct copy of the American M1911: in the M1914 the finger piece of the slide stop was lengthened. Ammunition is the 11.25 mm round which is identical to the .45ACP and the weapons were manufactured by Kongsberg Vaapenfabrikk: all other details are as in the Colt entry.

0.45 in SIG — SAUER P220 PISTOL (SWITZERLAND/GERMANY)

This entry relates to the version of the P220 pistol designed for use with 0.45ACP ammunition. A fuller description of the P220 family is given in the corresponding 9 mm entry: and apart from the calibre, a slight difference in weight (about 30 grams) and the use of a 7-round (instead of 8-round) magazine the data in that entry are applicable also to the 0.45 versions. Production of this version is scheduled for January 1977.

One of the most widely-used and widely-copied pistols, the Colt M1911A1 is derived from the M1911 which was adopted after troop trials competing with the Savage design in 1911 and remained in service unaltered until 1936. The alterations which produced the A1 version were minor changes to the grip, trigger, grip safety and hammer spur: in all essentials the weapon still in service today is the same as that adopted in 1911.

The method of operation involves a short recoil movement of the barrel and slide together, at the end of which the ribs on the top of the barrel, which have been engaged in the ceiling of the slide, are disengaged by the action of a pivoted link which couples the barrel to the receiver. The action of this link is both to pull the barrel down to free it from the slide and to halt its rearward motion; whereupon the continuing movement of the slide opens the breech, extracts the spent case and ejects it, compresses the return spring and cocks the hammer. The return spring then drives the slide forwards: if the magazine is empty the slide's motion will be arrested; otherwise a round will be chambered, the extractor on the face of the breech block will enter the extraction groove at the rear of the cartridge and, as the breech closes, the barrel will be driven forward with the slide and locked to it by the action of the pivoted link.

Safety arrangements are extensive. A manual safety, when operated, locks the hammer and sear to the receiver: a grip safety, when not operated, inhibits trigger movement. A disconnector prevents the trigger mechanism from operating until the slide is fully forward and the trigger has been released from the previous firing: there is also a half-cock bent on the hammer which enables the pistol to be

M1911 pistol *(RSAF)*.

carried in safety with a round in the chamber and enables the sear to catch the hammer before it reaches the firing pin if for some reason the sear slips off the main bent. Finally, the firing pin is shorter than the hole in which it is housed and is spring retracted: it will thus fire the round only if struck hard from the rear.

Ammunition: .45 Ball 1911 is the standard round. There are also blank and dummy rounds, a tracer (M26) and the High Density Shot M261 which contains 16 round shot in a bullet-shaped sabot

Operation: Short recoil, self-loading. See text

Magazine: 7-round detachable box

Sights: Blade foresight; U-notch rear

Rate of fire: 35 rounds/min

Effective range: 50 m

Total length: 22 cm (barrel 13 cm)

Weight: 1.1 kg empty; 1.3 kg loaded

Date introduced: 1911 and 1936

Manufacturers: Currently Colt. Formerly Colt, Ithaca, Remington, Springfield and Union Switch. Made under licence in Argentina and Norway. Extensively copied elsewhere.

Status: Currently in service in the USA and in most countries receiving or having received US military aid.

Colt 0.45in M1911A1 *(RSAF)*.

This weapon is an all-steel version of the Colt Commander which in turn was a derivative of the M1911A1 designed to meet a requirement for a lighter pistol for the non-military market. The Combat Commander was introduced in 1971 and is made in .45ACP, .38 Special and 9 mm Parabellum calibres. It has a shorter (108 mm) barrel than the M1911A1 and weighs about 0.2 kg less. The magazine of the .45 version holds seven rounds, as does the M1911A1, but the two smaller-calibre versions have 9-round magazines.

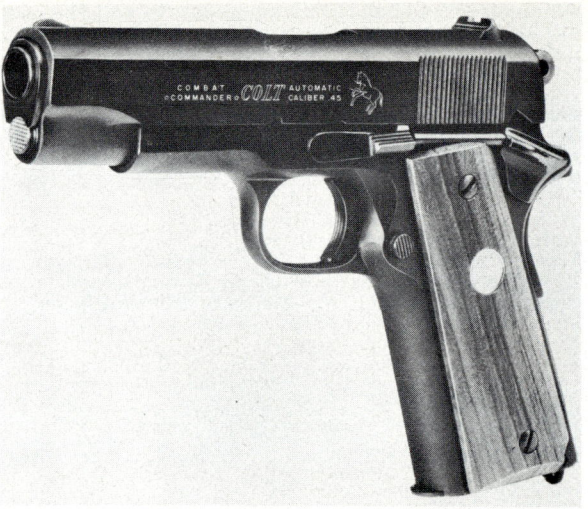

Colt Combat Commander in 0.45in calibre.

MACHINE PISTOLS

This blowback operated weapon combines the operational functions of an automatic pistol and a sub-machine gun. It fires the readily-available .32 Colt ACP which has made it an attractive export proposition, notably in Africa. An inertial cyclic rate reducer holds the rate of fire down to 840 rounds/min on normal automatic. The weapon has a folding stock, which makes it convenient for handling by armoured vehicle crews, can be fitted optionally with a bayonet, a silencer and a night sight and can be carried in a hip or shoulder holster. A choice of magazines is also available. Reported variants include a 9 mm x 18 version and a type incorporating a 3-round burst fire control.

Skorpion Vz61 machine pistol.

Ammunition: 7.65 mm (.32ACP)
Operation: Blowback, selective fire
Magazine: 10-round or 20-round detachable box
Sights: Protected cylindrical post foresight; flip rear sight with 75 or 150 m notches.
Rate of fire: Normal cyclic 840 rounds/min; 950 rounds/min when fitted with silencer; single shots 40 rounds/min
Effective range: 50 m with stock folded; 200 m with stock extended

Lengths: Stock extended: 51.5 cm; stock folded: 27 cm; barrel 11 cm; silencer 22 cm; gun with silencer and stock extended: 71.5 cm
Weights: Gun without magazine: 1.6 kg; 20-round magazine loaded: 0.4 kg
Manufacturer: State ordnance factories
Status: In service with Czechoslovakian forces and in several other countries. No longer manufactured.

This weapon is similar in concept to the Czech Skorpion and Russian Stechkin and combines the characteristics of a self-loading pistol and a fully automatic sub-machine gun in a compass that is small enough to enable it to be fired using only one hand. Conversion to two-handed use is effected by swivelling down and locking the forward grip and, if required, unfolding the built-in shoulder stock. The Wz63 is a blowback-operated weapon, firing from the open breech position, and it has a trigger mechanism which enables the firer to select single shots or fire by taking a light or heavy trigger pressure. It fires the Russian 9 mm x 18 round.

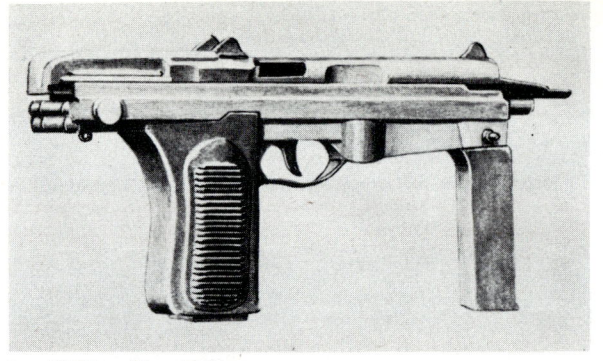

9mm Wz63 machine pistol.

Ammunition: 9 mm x 18
Operation: Blowback with selective fire
Magazine: 25-round or 40-round detachable box
Sights: Blade foresight; rear flip aperture 100/200 m
Rate of fire: Single shots 40 rounds/min; automatic 75 rounds/min; cyclic rate 600 rounds/min
Effective range: Stock retracted, 40 m; stock extended, 200 m
Total length: 33.5 cm or 60.5 cm with stock extended; barrel, 15 cm
Weight: 1.8 kg with empty 25-round magazine
Date introduced: 1963
Manufacturer: State factories
Status: No longer produced but in service with Polish forces.

SUB-MACHINE GUNS

This is a version of the 9 mm MP5 family of SMG which Heckler and Koch have made in 5.56 mm calibre. It is believed not to be in service anywhere yet. Details of general characteristics can be found in the corresponding 9 mm entry; the following data are peculiar to this version which is avaialable only with a telescopic stock.

Ammunition: 5.56 mm x 45
Magazine: 40-round detachable box
Rate of fire: Single shot 40 rounds/min; automatic 160 rounds/min; cyclic 600 rounds/min
Effective range: 400 m
Length: Stock extended, 75.5 cm; stock retracted, 56.5 cm; barrel 22.5 cm
Weight: 3.2 kg empty; 4.0 kg loaded
Status: Production.

5.56mm HK53 SMG.

5.56 mm HECKLER AND KOCH HK53 KL SMG

(GERMANY — BRD)

This is a derivative of the Heckler and Koch HK53 developed specially for use with the US Mechanized Infantry Combat Vehicle (MICV) as a fire port weapon (FPW). Designed to give close-in cover to deal with infantry approaching below the minimum depression zone of the vehicle machine gun it differs from the HK53 in the design of the forward portion which is compatible with the firing port, and from all other HK weapons in firing from an open breech position. This arrangement has the negligible disadvantage (in the circumstances) of increasing the lock time, but has the important advantage of giving improved heat dissipation properties to the barrel. The barrel is detachable.

HK53 KL.

This is a blowback-operated weapon with a very high rate of fire and a large magazine capacity. Fitted with a combined muzzle brake and compensator, it is said to have virtually no recoil muzzle blast or barrel climb. A 7.5 cm group at 18 m is said to be a reasonable performance after a little training. The butt is detachable.

Ammunition: .22 Long
Operation: Blowback; selective fire
Magazine: 177-round drum
Rate of fire: 1680 rounds/min cyclic
Effective range: 90 m (maximum practical 160 m)
Lengths: With butt, 90 cm; without butt, 64. 5 cm
Weight: Empty 3.9 kg; loaded 4.5 kg
Manufacturer: Voere GmbH
Status: Production.

7.62 mm TYPE 50 SMG

This is the Chinese copy of the Russian PPSh-41 SMG. The resemblance between the two weapons is so close that it is necessary here only to itemise the outward differences. All the Chinese weapons have a 35-round box magazine wherea some Russian models use a drum magazine. All Chinese weapons have an aperture rear sight. Finally the Chinese models are, of course, marked with Chinese characters. Present status is not known accurately, but the weapons have been widely distributed among Chinese and affiliated forces. General performance details will be found in the corresponding Russian entry.

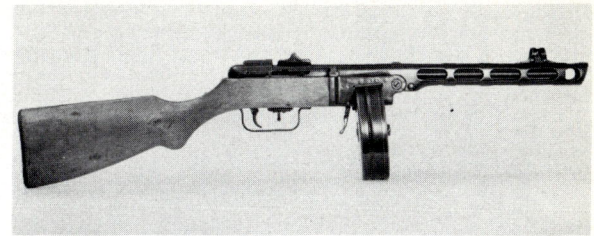

7.62mm Type 50 SMG *(RMCS)*.

This is a Chinese copy of the Russian PPS-43 SMG. At one time this weapon was thought to be called the Type 54 SMG but this is now known to be incorrect. Apart from the differences in markings there are no known differences between the Chinese copies and the Russian originals. Performance details are given in the Russian entry.

7.62mm Type 43 copy SMG *(RMCS)*.

7.62 mm TYPE 54 SMG

This designation was at one time applied to the weapon which is now known to be correctly described as the Type 43 SMG — under which heading further information will be found.

7.62 mm TYPE 64 SILENCED SMG

This weapon is the only SMG known to have been designed and built in China but its design relies heavily on earlier European weapons. The Type 64 is blowback-operated with a fluted chamber to ease extraction of the spent case and a Bren-type trigger mechanism. A Maxim-type suppressor is used: the front third of the barrel is perforated to release propellant gases into a surrounding tube. This projects some 15 cm beyond the end of the barrel and carries a stack of dished and perforated baffles through which the bullet must pass and which dissipate the energy of the emerging gases: they also prevent muzzle flash. The weapon has a folding stock.

Ammunition: 7.62 mm x 25 'P' Ball
Operation: Blowback; selective fire
Magazine: 30-round detachable box
Sights: Blade foresight; rear notch
Rate of fire: Cyclic 1315 rounds/min
Effective range: 135 m
Total length: Stock open, 84.5 cm; stock closed, 63.5 cm; barrel, 24.5 cm
Weight: 3.4 kg empty
Manufacturer: State factories
Status: No longer produced. In service in China and Vietnam at least.

Chinese Type 64 silenced SMG.

These two weapons are almost identical with the 9 mm Vz 23 and Vz 25 weapons except for the difference in calibre. They are visually distinguishable by their phosphated metal finish which replaces the black of the earlier weapons and their pistol grips which point slightly forward. Detailed information on the Vz 23 and Vz 25 will be found among the 9 mm entries: significant points of difference are summarised briefly below.

Ammunition: 7.62 mm x 25 M48
Magazine: 32-round detachable box
Date introduced: 1953
Status: Certainly in first-line service until 1962 and still used in Czechoslovakia. No longer made.

7.62 mm M48 SMG

(HUNGARY)

This is a Hungarian copy of the Russian PPSh-41 SMG. It is well-made and well-finished and has the same characteristics as the Russian original which is separately described.

Manufacturer: State factories
Status: Obsolescent in Hungarian service.

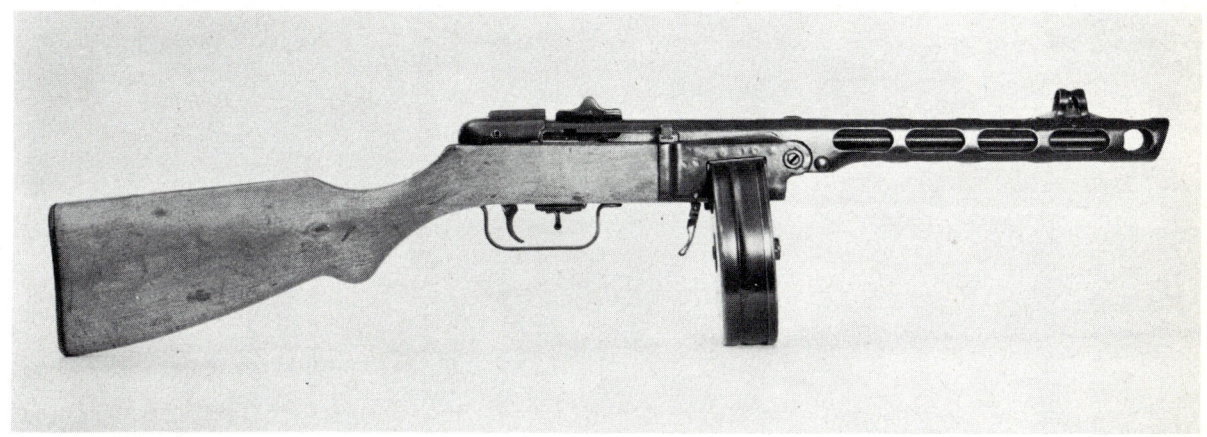

Hungarian 48M *(RMCS)*.

This is a direct copy of the 7.62 mm Russian PPSh-41 and was made in Pyongyang in 1949-50. When US troops captured and briefly held the city, production was hastily removed northwards where it remained in operation until 1955. The weapon is still in service with North Korean forces and may be distinguished from the Russian original by its aperture rear sight and the star and circle marking on the receiver.

7.62 mm PPS-42 AND PPS-43 SMG

(USSR)

These weapons are the first and second versions of a SMG designed to meet an urgent need for a small automatic weapon for tank crews and paratroops. The PPS-42 was designed, built and tested during the siege of Leningrad and the PPS-43 was a shorter and further simplified version of an already simple design. The external differences are small.

Blowback-operated, the weapon fires only in the automatic mode. It uses a 35-round curved box magazine that is not interchangeable with that of the PPSh-41 and its folding metal stock is unusual in that it lies on top of the magazine when folded. A combined muzzle brake and compensator is fitted.

PPS-43 7.62mm SMG *(RMCS)*.

Ammunition: 7.62 mm x 25 'P' pistol or 7.63 mm Mauser
Operation: Blowback; automatic only
Magazine: 35-round box
Sights: Post foresight; flip notch rear 100/200 m
Rate of fire: Cyclic 650-700 rounds/min
Effective range: 200 m
Lengths: Stock extended, 90.5 cm (PPS-42) or 82 cm; stock retracted, 64 cm or 61.5 cm; barrel, 27.5 cm or 25.5 cm
Weight: Loaded, 3.9 kg (PPS-42) or 3.6 kg
Manufacturer: State factories
Status: No longer made or in USSR service but certainly still used in South East Asia and probably elsewhere. A close copy was made in China and a similar weapon with a wooden stock in Poland (M43/52).

This SMG is now obsolete in the Red Army but was supplied in quantity to many other areas and has been widely copied; so that it is still very much a current weapon. It was designed in 1941 and was in production in 1942 and more than five million were made before the end of the war.

PPSh-41 is a blowback-operated, selective fire weapon with a wooden butt and a chromium-plated barrel. Early models had a tangent leaf rearsight but this was replaced from late 1942 by a 100/200 m flip sight. The barrel is surounded by a vented jacket which extends beyond the muzzle and acts both as a muzzle brake and as a compensator. The change lever is a sliding catch inside the trigger guard and the safety is a latch on the cocking handle which can thus be locked, in slots in the cocking way, in either the forward or the cocked position.

The magazine is either a 71-round drum with two feed lips or a 35-round, slightly curved, box. The drum magazines could not necessarily be transferred satisfactorily from one gun to another and were serially numbered in the same sequence as the guns.

PPSh-41 with 71-round drum *(RMCS)*.

Ammunition: 7.62 mm x 25 'P' pistol
Operation: Blowback; selective fire
Magazine: 71-round drum or 35-round box
Sights: Post foresight usually protected; early models tangent rear sight 50-500 m; later models flip notch 100/200 m
Rate of fire: Single shots 40 rounds/min; automatic 105 rounds/min; cyclic 900 rounds/min
Effective range: 200 m
Total length: 84 cm (barrel 27 cm)
Weight: Loaded, 4.3 kg (35 rounds) or 5.4 kg (71 rounds)
Date introduced: 1942
Manufacturer: State factories in the USSR and satellite countries some of which made variants which are described separately
Status: Obsolete in the USSR but still in service in various parts of the world. It has been seen recently in service in the Middle East and with the East German Border Guards, has been manufactured in China, Hungary, Iran and North Korea and supplied to Vietnam and neighbouring countries.

PPSh-41 with 35-round box magazine *(RMCS)*.

129

This is a Vietnamese modification of the Chinese Type 50 SMG — itself a copy of the Russian PPSh-41. The major modifications comprise removal of the upward folding stock and its replacement by a sliding stock similar to that used on the French MAT 49: shortening and tapering the barrel jacket; removing the muzzle brake/compensator; reshaping the lower receiver and adding a pistol grip to it; and mounting the foresight on the barrel. The operating mechanisms have not been changed.

Ammunition: 7.62 mm x 25 Pistol 'P', or PRC Pistol, or 7.63 mm Mauser
Operation: Blowback; selective fire
Magazine: 35-round detachable box
Sights: Post foresight; flip notch rear 100/200 m
Rate of fire: Cyclic 700 rounds/min
Effective range: 200 m
Lengths: Stock extended, 75.5 cm; stock retracted, 57 cm; barrel 27 cm
Weight: 4.1 kg loaded
Manufacturer: Modified in local workshops
Status: No longer made but probably still in service.

Vietnamese K-50M SMG *(RSAF)*.

7.62 mm MODIFIED MAT 49 SMG (VIETNAM)

During the French campaign in Indo-China a large number of French MAT-49 9 mm SMG were captured by the Vietnamese. Many of these weapons were subsequently converted to fire the Russian 7.62 mm x 25 pistol cartridge. The main features of the original weapon were retained but the replacement barrel was some 7 cm longer than that of the MAT-49.

The modifications were carried out in Vietnam and some of the weapons are probably still in service.

Vietnamese modification of French MAT49 *(J. Smith)*.

7.62 mm M49 AND M49/57 SMG

These weapons are versions of the Russian PPSh-41 SMG and resemble it fairly closely in operational detail though the manufacturing methods used are different. Observable different features of the Yugoslav weapons are the large push-through safety in front of the trigger guard, and the small circular holes in the barrel jacket in place of long slots: a different buffer assembly, resembling that of the Beretta M38A, is another feature.

Neither weapon can accept the Russian drum magazine but they will accept the box magazines from the PPSh-41 and the Chinese Type 50 as well as the 35-round Yugoslav magazine.

There are no important differences between the M49 and the M49/57.

Ammunition: 7.62 mm x 25 Pistol 'P' or 7.63 mm Mauser
Operation: Blowback; selective fire
Magazine: 35-round curved box
Sights: Blade foresight; flip notch rear 100/200 m
Rate of fire: Single shots 40 rounds/min; automatic 120 rounds/min; cyclic 700 rounds/min
Effective range: 200 m
Total length: 87 cm (barrel 27.5 cm)
Weight: 3.9 kg empty; 4.5 kg loaded
Manufacturer: Crvena Zastava
Status: No longer made. In Yugoslav Army service.

Yugoslav M49/57 SMG.

132

7.62 mm M56 SMG

This SMG is similar in appearance to the German MP40 and incorporates the better features of that weapon and the M49. Blowback-operated with selective fire it has a cocking handle that can be locked in slots at each end of the cocking way. It has a folding stock like that of the MP40, accepts a knife pattern bayonet and has a magazine which is interchangeable with that of the M49.

Ammunition: 7.62 mm Pistol 'P' or 7.63 mm Mauser
Operation: Blowback; selective fire
Magazine: 32-round detachable box
Sights: Hooded blade foresight; flip notch rear 100/200 m
Rate of fire: Cyclic 600 rounds/min
Effective range: 200 m
Lengths: Stock extended, 87 cm; stock folded, 59 cm; barrel 25 cm
Weight: 3.1 kg
Manufacturer: Crvena Zastava
Status: No longer made. In service with Yugoslav forces.

Yugoslav troops with the M56.

Although no longer manufactured or in French military service this early weapon certainly found its way into the war in Vietnam and may be found elsewhere. It is the only SMG to fire the 7.65 mm Long cartridge and, although accurate, lacks penetrating power. A unique feature of the design is the spring-buffered sear; this is designed to prevent damage by the bolt which travels well behind the sear on the rearward half-cycle and has thus acquired considerable energy when it reaches the sear on the forward half-cycle.

First produced in 1939, the MAS 38 continued in production throughout the German occupation.

Ammunition: 7.62 mm Long
Operation: Blowback; automatic only
Magazine: 32-round detachable box
Sights: Blade foresight; notch rear
Rate of fire: Cyclic 600 rounds/min
Effective range: 150 m
Total length: 73.5 cm (barrel 22.5 cm)
Weight: 2.9 kg empty; 3.4 kg loaded
Date introduced: 1939
Manufacturer: Manufacture d'Armes de St. Etienne
Status: No longer made or in French service. Was in service in Vietnam recently and may still be encountered.

7.65mm MAS Model 38 *(RMCS)*.

9 mm PAM SMG

(ARGENTINA)

There were two versions of this weapon, PAM 1 and PAM 2, both modelled on the US M3A1 but differing from it in calibre and in being shorter and lighter. PAM 1 was capable of automatic fire only: PAM 2 could provide selective fire. Both have now been withdrawn from service in Argentina but may well still exist.

Ammunition: 9 mm Parabellum
Operation: Blowback automatic (PAM 1) or selective (PAM 2)
Magazine: 30-round box
Sights: Blade foresight; flip notch rear 100/200 m
Rate of fire: 210 rounds/min at cyclic rate of 450 rounds/min
Effective range: 200 m
Lengths: Stock extended, 72.5 cm; stock retracted, 54 cm; barrel 20 cm
Weight: 3.3 kg unloaded; 3.6 kg loaded
Manufacturer: Fabrica Militar, Rosario
Status: No longer made or in Argentine service.

9mm PAM 1 SMG.

This is the current Argentine SMG. It features a wrap-around bolt which encloses 18 cm of the 29 cm barrel when closed. It is a blowback weapon with selective fire capability. The cocking handle is on the left and there is a slide cover to keep dirt out of the cocking slot. There are two versions of the SMG, one having a fixed plastic butt and the other a sliding butt similar to that of the US M3.

Ammunition: 9 mm Parabellum
Operation: Blowback with selective fire
Magazine: 25-round box
Sights: Pillar foresight; flip aperture rear 50/100 m
Rate of fire: SS 50 rounds/min; automatic 100 rounds/min; cyclic 650 rounds/min
Effective range: 200 m
Lengths: Fixed butt, 70 cm; sliding butt extended, 69.5 cm; retracted, 52.5 cm; barrel 29 cm
Weight: 3.6 kg empty; 3.9 kg loaded
Manufacturer: Fabrica Militar, Rosario
Status: In production and service.

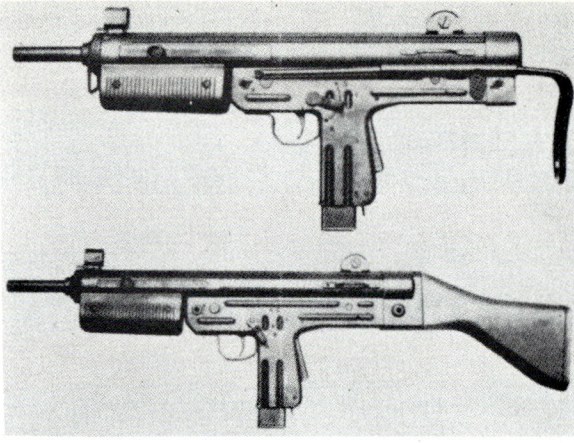

PA3-DM SMG.

9 mm AUSTEN SMG

(AUSTRALIA)

Two versions of the Austen — Australian Sten — were produced during the Second World War to overcome a shortage of British-supplied weapons. Derived from the Sten but incorporating some features of the German MP40, both were blowback weapons of simple design with folding butts. Both overlapped in production with the Owen SMG and may possibly still be encountered — particularly the Mk II, details of which are given below.

DATA (Mk II)
Ammunition: 9 mm Parabellum
Operation: Blowback, selective fire
Magazine: 28-round box
Sights: Blade foresight; 100-yard aperture rear
Rate of fire: Single shots, 40 rounds/min; automatic, 120 rounds/min; cyclic 500 rounds/min
Effective range: 200 m
Total length: Butt extended, 84.5 cm; butt folded, 55 cm; barrel 20 cm
Weight: 4.7 kg loaded
Date introduced: 1944
Manufacturer: Diecasters Ltd. and W.J. Carmichael & Co
Status: Obsolete. See text.

9mm Austen MkI *(RMCS)*.

This wartime weapon was produced between 1941 and 1944 and was the subject of a refurbishment programme in the 1950s but has long since been withdrawn from first-line Australian service. Some were still in use during the war in Vietnam, however, and may still survive. Others may be found in reserve units. Recognisable by its forward-sloping top-mounted magazine the Owen was a sturdy blowback-operated weapon with a well-enclosed mechanism. The Mk 1/43 version was lighter than the original Mk 1/42: and a later version had provision for mounting a bayonet. All had quick-release barrels and were fitted with muzzle compensators.

DATA (Mk1/43)
Ammunition: 9 mm Parabellum
Operation: Blowback; selective fire
Magazine: 28-round box
Sights: Blade foresight; offset rear aperture
Rate of fire: Single shots 40 rounds/min; automatic 120 rounds/min; cyclic 700 rounds/min
Effective range: 200 m
Total length: 81.5 cm (excluding bayonet); barrel 25 cm
Weight: 4.9 kg loaded
Manufacturer: Lysaght Newcastle Works
Status: Obsolescent. See text.

Owen MkI/42 SMG *(RMCS)*.

Owen Mk II/43 *(RSAF)*.

138

9 mm F1 SMG

This is the current Australian Army SMG. It is a blowback-operated weapon with a left-hand non-reciprocating cocking handle which can be locked to the breeched block if required to clear dirt. The straight-through butt and top-mounted magazine necessitate a rather high offset rear sight. There is no forward grip, but the sling swivel and a guard for the ejector slot prevent the firer from putting his hand in a silly place. There is provision for fixing a bayonet and the magazine is interchangeable with UK and Canadian equivalents. Several of the weapon's components are common with those of the L1A1 Rifle.

9mm F1 SMG.

Ammunition: 9 mm Parabellum
Operation: Blowback; selective fire
Magazine: 34-round box
Sights: Offset blade foresight; offset hinged plate with aperture at rear
Rate of fire: Single shots 40 rounds/min; automatic 120 rounds/min; cyclic 600-640 rounds/min
Effective range: 200 m
Total length: 71.5 cm (barrel 21.5 cm)
Weight: 4.3 kg loaded (with bayonet)
Date introduced: 1962
Manufacturer: Small Arms Factory (Lithgow)
Status: In Australian Army service.

This blowback-operated weapon uses a wrap-around bold system similar to that of the UZI which it resembles. It fires by the advanced primer ignition system: that is the primer is detonated by the firing pin, while the round is being chambered, as soon as the friction between the cartridge and the chamber is sufficient. Some of the rearward force is thus dissipated in halting the bolt, and the wrap-around prevents any escaping gas from striking the firer. Other features are the combined pistol-grip and magazine housing, the telescopic stock and the use of different trigger pressures to select different types of fire. The forward end of the sling is attached to the cocking piece and may be used to cock the weapon. The safety catch may be operated from either side.

9mm Steyr MP69 SMG *(RMCS)*.

Ammunition: 9 mm x 19 Parabellum
Operation: Blowback; selective fire
Magazine: 25-round detachable box
Sights: Protected post foresight; 50 m aperture rear
Rate of fire: Single shots 50 rounds/min; automatic 100 rounds/min; cyclic 550 rounds/min
Effective range: 200 m
Total length: Butt extended 67.5 cm; butt retracted 47 cm; barrel 26 cm
Weight: 3.5 kg loaded
Manufacturer: Steyr-Daimler-Puch
Status: In production. In service with Austrian forces and on offer elsewhere.

9 mm MITRAILLETTE VIGNERON M2 SMG

(BELGIUM)

This SMG was first issued to Belgian troops in 1953 and is still a reserve service weapon. Blowback-operated with selective fire it is unusual in having a relatively long barrel with a compensator and a retractable wire stock with a choice of three length positions. There is a grip safety in the pistol grip.

Mitraillette Vigneron *(RSAF)*.

Ammunition: 9 mm Parabellum
Operation: Blowback; selective fire
Magazine: 32-round box
Sights: Blade foresight; 50 m aperture rear
Rate of fire: Single shots 40 rounds/min; automatic 120 rounds/min; cyclic 620 rounds/min
Effective range: 200 m
Total length: Butt fully extended, 88.5 cm; butt retracted 70.5 cm; barrel 30.5 cm
Weight: 3.3 kg loaded
Date introduced: 1953
Manufacturer: SA Précision Liègeoise
Status: No longer in production. In service with Belgian forces. Formerly in service in the Belgian Congo and probably still used in the area.

(BURMA)

9 mm BA52 SMG

This is a copy of the Italian TZ45 which appeared at the end of the Second World War. Blowback-operated and giving automatic fire only, it is simple both in design and manufacture. The vertical box magazine is used as a forward grip and is fitted with a grip safety which locks the bolt unless grasped for firing. The weapon has a retractable stock and is fitted with a small muzzle brake.

Ammunition: 9 mm
Operation: Blowback; automatic only
Magazine: 40-round detachable box
Sights: Blade foresight; fixed aperture rear
Rate of fire: 100-120 rounds/min automatic
Effective range: 100 m
Total length: Stock extended 81.5 cm; stock retracted, 56 cm
Weight: 7.3 kg loaded
Status: Probably still in service in parts of South-East Asia.

9 mm C1 SMG   (CANADA)

This is a slightly modified version of what is generally known as the Sterling SMG and has been in service in the UK in various marks since its adoption as the L2A1 in 1953. Some early models were supplied to Canada in unmodified form; but the weapons currently in Canadian service were made by Canadian Arsenals. The main differences between the Canadian and British weapons are in the smaller magazine (30 rounds) with a conventional magazine follower and provision for fitting the FAL rifle type of bayonet instead of the British No. 5 bayonet. Otherwise most parts are interchangeable.

Canadian 9mm C1 SMG *(RSAF)*.

Ammunition: 9 mm Parabellum
Operation: Blowback; selective fire
Magazine: 30-round box; A 10-round magazine has been produced
Sights: Blade foresight; 100 m aperture rear
Rate of fire: Single shots 40 rounds/min; automatic 120 rounds/min; cyclic 550 rounds/min
Effective range: 200 m
Total length: Butt extended, 68.5 cm; butt folded, 49.5 cm; barrel, 20 cm
Weight: 3.5 kg loaded
Date introduced: 1958
Manufacturer: Canadian Arsenals
Status: In service with Canadian armed forces.

(CZECHOSLOVAKIA)

9 mm VZ 23 AND 25 SMG

These two weapons differ only in that the Vz23 has a fixed wooden stock and Vz25 a folding metal stock. Operation is by blowback with selective fire determined by trigger pressure and a wrap-around bolt is used. This bolt has an ejection port cut in it so that the mechanism is closed to dirt except when this port coincides with that in the receiver casing. The use of the weapons in Czechoslovakia was discontinued in the early 1950s in favour of similar weapons, Vz 24 and Vz 26, in 7.62 mm calibre. These SMG are separately described. In all four weapons a magazine loader is attached to the right side of the foregrip and is used with 8-round clips.

Czech 9mm Vz23 *(RSAF)*.

Ammunition: 9 mm x 19 Parabellum
Operation: Blowback; selective fire by trigger pressure
Magazine: 24-round or 40-round detachable box
Sights: Hooded barleycorn front; notch rear
Rate of fire: Cyclic 650 rounds/min
Effective range: 200 m
Total length: Wooden stock (Vz 23), 67.5 cm; metal stock
extended (Vz 25) 68.5 cm; stock folded 44.5 cm; barrel 28.5
cm
Weight: Vz 23, 3.3 kg; Vz 25, 3.5 kg empty
Date introduced: 1951
Manufacturer: Ceskoslovenska Zbrojovka, Brno
Status: No longer manufactured. No longer in Czech military
service. Supplied to Cuba and Syria where some are
probably still used. Extensively used in the Nigerian civil
war. 7.62 mm weapons Vz 24 and Vz 26 are still in service in
Czechoslovakia.

9mm Vz25 *(RSAF)*.

This is a 9 mm Parabellum version of the Chinese Type 36 SMG — and hence of the US M3A1. It was introduced in 1948 but it is not definitely known to be in service now. Apart from the calibre the SMG has the same characteristics as the 0.45 M3A1 and details are given in the American entry for that weapon.

9 mm HOVEA M49 SMG   (DENMARK)

This weapon was designed in Sweden at the Husqvarna arms factory and competed with the Carl Gustav weapon in arms trials at which the latter weapon (the M45) was selected. The Hovea was preferred by the Danish authorities, however, and they purchased a quantity together with a manufacturing licence; and Danish-built weapons are still in service with Danish forces. The weapon was originally designed to take the Finnish 50-round magazine but this was subsequently replaced by the 36-round Carl Gustav box. Fitted with a rectangular folding stock the Hovea bears a superficial resemblance to both the Carl Gustav M45 and the Madsen weapons.

Ammunition: 9 mm Parabellum
Operation: Blowback; fully automatic only
Magazine: 36-round detachable box (see text)
Sights: Blade front; U-notch flip rear 100/200 m
Rate of fire: Cyclic 600 rounds/min
Effective range: 150 m
Total length: Stock extended, 81 cm; stock folded, 55 cm; barrel 21.5 cm
Weight: 3.4 kg empty; 4.0 kg loaded
Manufacturer: Haerens Vabenarsanalet
Status: In service with Danish forces.

A series of SMG — M46, M50, M51 and two marks of an M53 — have been produced in Denmark by Madsen. All are similar and simple in design and have the same rectangular folding stock. All are blowback-operated and use advanced primer ignition, the round being fired just before the bolt finishes its forward travel. All save the M53 Mk II will fire only fully automatic and all have a grip safety mounted behind the magazine housing which must be depressed for the weapon to fire.

A 32-round box magazine is used and this can be filled easily by using a magazine filler which is enclosed in the pistol grip: this fits over the top of the (detached) magazine and depresses the strong spring while each round is loaded. Unfortunately, to remove the filler from the pistol grip the two halves of the gun must be unscrewed and opened up, thus putting the gun out of action for a time; and because of this hand filling of the magazine is often attempted — laborious and awkward as it is. The magazines of the various models are different: those of the M46, M50 and M51 are straight-sided and have a single-position feed design; whereas the two M53 models use a curved box with a two-position feed arrangement.

Other differences involve the cocking handles and barrel nuts. The M46 had a handle shaped to the receiver: later models have a small knob on top of the receiver. The M53 has a knurled cylindrical barrel nut which screws on the barrel: the earlier models have a grooved nut fitting on the receiver.

Madsen M53 Mk2.

DATA (Generally applicable to M53)
Ammunition: 9 mm Parabellum
Operation: Blowback; M53 Mk II selective; M46, M50 and
M53 Mk I automatic only
Magazine: 32-round box (see text)
Sights: Blade foresight; aperture rear
Rate of fire: Selective (M53 Mk II) 45 rounds/min;
automatic 100 rounds/min (if magazine available); cyclic
550 rounds/min
Effective range: 150 m
Length: Stock extended 79.5 cm; stock folded 53 cm; barrel
20 cm
Weight: 3.2 kg empty
Manufacturer: Madsen
Status: In service with Danish police forces and with the
armed forces of several South American states. Made under
licence in 0.45 in calibre by INA in Brazil. Also found in
South-East Asia.

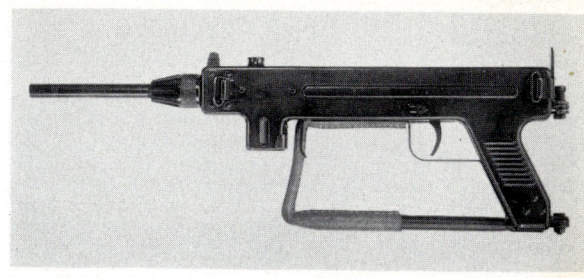

9mm Madsen Model 50 *(RMCS)*.

Although of pre-war design and expensively made, this weapon continues in service with Finnish forces. The Finns were European leaders in SMG design and the M31 is the successor of the Lahti 1926 model in 7.65 mm Parabellum. It was made by Oy Tikkakoski in Finland, built under licence in Sweden and Switzerland and sold to Norway. It is blowback-operated with selective fire and all the working parts are machined from the solid. The box magazine was unusual in having two columns of rounds, with separate follower springs, feeding a single exit. There was also a drum magazine which was subsequently copied by the Russians for the PPD 34/38.

9mm Suomi M31.

Ammunition: 9 mm Parabellum
Operation: Blowback; selective fire
Magazine: 50-round box or 71-round drum; possibly also the Carl Gustav 36-round box
Sights: Blade foresight; rear adjustable 100-300 m
Rate of Fire: Cyclic 800 rounds/min
Effective range: 200 m
Total length: 87 cm (barrel 32 cm)
Weight: 4.7 kg empty; 7.1 kg with loaded drum
Manufacturer: Oy Tikkakoski
Status: In service with Finnish forces.

9 mm M44 SMG   (FINLAND)

This is a copy of the 7.62 mm Russian PPS-43 SMG made in Finland for the 9 mm Parabellum round. A large quantity was made in 1944 and the weapon is still in Finnish Army service, having been modified to take the Carl Gustav 36-round magazine as well as the 71-round drum with which it was originally fitted. The mechanical and performance data of this weapon differ slightly from the Russian original and are set out below.

Ammunition: 9 mm x 19 Parabellum
Operation: Blowback; automatic fire only
Magazine: 36-round Carl Gustav box or 71-round drum
Sights: Blade foresight; flip notch rear 100/200 m
Rate of fire: Cyclic 650 rounds/min
Effective range: 200 m
Total length: Stock extended, 83 cm; stock folded, 62 cm; barrel, 25 cm
Weight: Empty 2.9 kg; loaded 3.6 kg or 4.3 kg
Manufacturer: Oy Tikkakoski. Subsequently made at Oriedo as the Dux SMG
Status: No longer manufactured. In service with Finnish troops.

This weapon was designed, and subsequently adopted, as the standard French SMG, replacing the miscellany of 9 mm, 0.45 in and 7.65 mm weapons with which the French forces were equipped at the end of the Second World War. A conventional, blowback, automatic-only weapon it is unusual in having a magazine housing which can be folded forward to clip under the barrel: with the stock retracted also the weapon thus becomes very convenient to carry. Other features include an intermediate latching position for the retractable stock and a grip safety.

Ammunition: 9 mm Parabellum
Operation: Blowback; automatic only
Magazine: 32-round detachable box
Sights: Hooded blade foresight; flip aperture rear 100/200 m
Rate of fire: Cyclic 600 rounds/min
Effective range: 200 m
Total length: Stock extended, 71 cm; stock retracted, 46 cm; barrel, 23 cm
Weight: Empty 3.6 kg; loaded 4.8 kg
Date introduced: 1949
Manufacturer: Manufacture d'Armes de Tulle
Status: No longer in production. Standard weapon in the French armed forces and to be found elsewhere in former French territory.

9mm MAT 49 SMG *(RMCS)*.

152

9 mm GEVARM & GEVELOT SMG   (FRANCE)

This is a simple and sturdy weapon designed for satisfactory operation in a wide range of climatic conditions. It is fitted with a simple retractable wire stock.

Ammunition: 9 mm Parabellum
Operation: Blowback
Magazine: 32-round detachable box
Sights: Blade foresight; flip rear 50/100 m
Rate of fire: Cyclic 600 rounds/min
Effective range: 100 m
Length: Stock retracted 50 cm; barrel 22 cm
Weight: Empty, 3.5 kg; loaded, 3.9 kg
Manufacturer: Gevarm & Gevelot
Status: Production

Commonly referred to, incorrectly, as 'Schmeisser' SMG, these weapons were in fact designed at Erma-Werke and the first, the MP38, was manufactured only by Erma. It incorporated a high proportion of machined parts and was costly to produce: the MP40 was a cheapened version suitable for mass production. The MP38/40 was the designation given to an MP38 fitted with the MP40 two-piece cocking handle to prevent it from firing when dropped. Two other variants were the MP40/I (sometimes called the MP41), which had a fixed wooden stock in place of the folding metal one, and the MP40/II which had twin 32-round magazines with a changeover device.

By far the commonest model, however, was the MP40 which, although no longer in German military service, still exists in large numbers in many parts of the world — not surprisingly since more than a million were made. It is a simple blowback automatic-only weapon with a relatively low rate of fire and, like the Sten, was one of the most widely-known weapons of the Second World War.

9mm MP38 *(RMCS)*.

Ammunition: 9 mm Parabellum
Operation: Blowback; automatic only
Magazine: 32-round detachable box; double box for MP 40/II
Sights: Hooded barleycorn foresight; flip notch rear 100/200 m
Rate of fire: Cyclic 500 rounds/min
Total length: Stock extended 83 cm; stock folded 63 cm; barrel 25 cm
Weight: 4.0 kg empty; 4.7 kg loaded; 5.5 kg loaded for MP 40/II
Manufacturer: Erma-Werke and many others
Status: No longer produced. In Austrian Army service and to be found in many other countries.

MP 40/II SMG *(RSAF)*.

These two weapons have a complicated history, part of which is recounted in the entry for the Finnish MP44. After the Second World War the manager of the Tikkakoski Arsenal took the designs of the MP44 out of Finland; and these later became the basis of the Dux 53 weapon which was purchased for the west German border guards and made by Mauser. A further stage of development led to the Dux 59 — an improvement on the 53 and less like the Russian PPS-43.

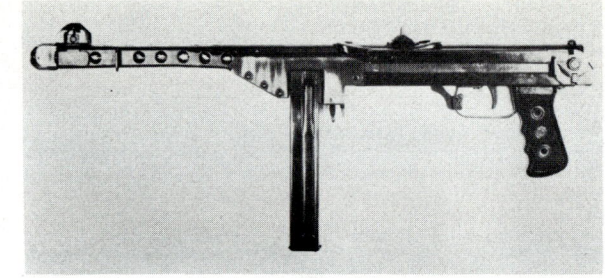

Dux 53 SMG.

Ammunition: 9 mm x 19 Parabellum
Operation: Blowback; automatic only
Magazine: Dux 53, 50-round Suomi Box; Dux 59, 32- or 40-round box
Sights: Blade foresight; flip notch rear 100/200 m
Rate of fire: Cyclic, 500 rounds/min
Effective range: 200 m
Total length: Stock extended, 82.5 cm (53) or 79 cm (59; stock folded, 61.5 cm (53) or 58 cm (59); barrel 25 cm
Weight: Empty, 3.6 kg (53) or 3.0 kg (59); loaded, 4.1 kg (53) or 3.6 kg (59)
Manufacturer: Mauser
Status: No longer made. Still used by German border guards.

Dux 59.

(GERMANY — BRD)

9 mm WALTHER MP-K AND MP-L SMG

These two weapons differ only in barrel length, the K (kurz) barrel being the shorter. Both are blowback-operated, with advanced primer ignition, have provision for selective fire, use 32-round box magazines, have folding stocks and can be fitted with silencers. An unusual sighting arrangement permits the upper aperture of the rear sight to be used with the top of the foresight protector to give the same setting as is obtained with the lower aperture and the normal foresight blade. This is intended to help the firer in poor light conditions.

Neither weapon has been adopted by any regular army but both are used by police and some naval forces.

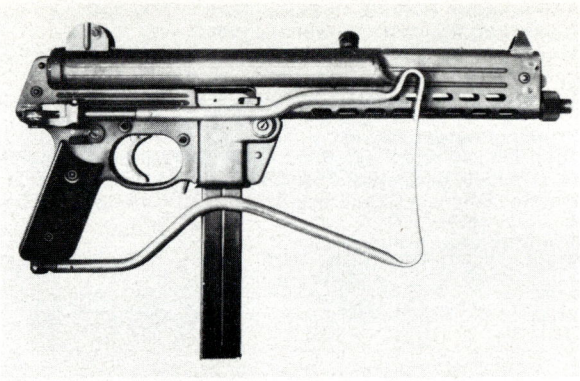

9mm Walther MP-L SMG.

Ammunition: 9 mm x 19 Parabellum
Operation: Blowback; selective fire
Magazine: 32-round detachable box
Sights: Blade foresight; 75 m notch and 125 m aperture rear (see text)
Rate of fire: Single shots 40 rounds/min; automatic 96 rounds/min; cyclic 550 rounds/min
Effective range: 100 m
Lengths: MP-K: stock open, 65.5 cm; stock closed, 37 cm; barrel 17 cm; MP-L: Stock open, 73.5 cm; stock closed, 45.5 cm; barrel 25.5 cm
Weights: MP-K: 3.0 kg empty; 3.4 kg loaded; MP-L: 3.2 kg empty; 3.6 kg loaded
Manufacturer: Carl Walther
Status: Used by German Police and some others (see text).

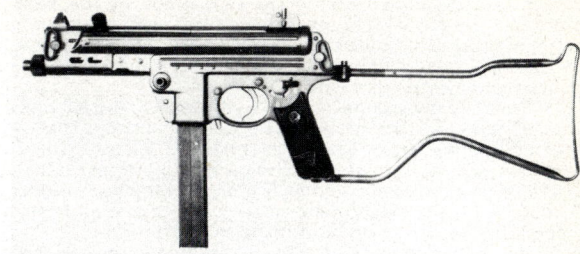

Walther MP-K.

(GERMANY — BRD)

This is a derivative of the G3 rifle made by the same manufacturers and uses the same roller-locking system to achieve delayed blowback. The SMG has for some time been in German police use and has been purchased by the military of several countries.

There are two versions of the 9 mm weapon: the A2 has a fixed plastic stock and the A3 has a telescopic stock. There is also a 5.56 mm version known as the HK53. All three have a selective fire facility, offer a choice of magazines holding 10,15 or 30 rounds and can be fitted with telescopic sights. A feature of the mechanism is that the gun fires from a closed bolt, which is unusual for a modern SMG.

A sub-calibre conversion unit is available to enable the 9 mm weapon to fire .22LR ammunition.

Heckler and Koch MP5 A3.

Ammunition: 9 mm x 19 Parabellum
Operation: Delayed blowback (rollers); selective fire
Magazine: Detachable box containing 10, 15 or 30 rounds
Sights: Fixed post foresight; rear notch for 100 m and apertures for 200, 300 and 400 m
Rate of fire: Single shots, 40-50 rounds/min; automatic, 100 rounds/min; cyclic, 650 rounds/min
Effective range: 400 m
Lengths: MP5-A2 total 68 cm; MP5-A3 Stock open 66 cm, stock closed 49 cm; barrel, 22.5 cm
Weights: Empty 2.5 kg (A2) or 2.6 kg; loaded with 30-round magazine, 2.9 kg (A2) or 3.0 kg
Manufacturer: Heckler and Koch
Status: In production and in police and some military service.

9 mm MP5 SD SMG

This is a silenced version of the MP5 weapon and is available in three versions, two of which offer the same choice of fixed or retractable stocks as the unsilenced weapon while the third has the stock replaced by a receiver end-cap.

The mechanism of the SD version is the same as that of the MP 5 but it is fitted with a drilled barrel surrounded by a cylindrical steel jacket containing a helix which absorbs some of the energy of the gases emerging through the holes and from the muzzle and reduces the emergent gas velocity below that of sound. Inevitably the loss of gas pressure causes a reduction in the muzzle velocity of the bullet.

Characteristics generally are similar to those of the MP5. Those that differ are summarised below.

MP5 SD SMG.

DATA (See also MP5)
Sights: Iron sights as MP5. Telescopic and image intensifier sights available
Effective range: 150 m
Length: Increased by 11 cm (not the barrel)
Weight: Increased by about 0.3 kg. Version without stock weighs about 0.3 kg less than the fixed stock version
Status: Production.

During the Indonesian confrontation with the UK in 1963 several locally-produced copies of European SMG were encountered in Indonesian service. Commonest among these were copies of the Italian Beretta and Spanish Star, but the Swedish Carl Gustav was also seen. Some of these weapons may well still exist.

Indonesian copy of the Beretta 38/49 *(RSAF)*.

Indonesian copy of the Spanish 9mm Star *(RSAF)*.

9 mm PM MODEL VII SMG

(INDONESIA)

This is an original Indonesian design produced by the Bandung Arsenal in 1957. Of conventional blowback design, it is reminiscent of the US M3 weapon in its sliding wire stock and in the design of the cover. It was fitted with a slotted jacket and a Beretta-type compensator.

Ammunition: 9 mm x 19 Parabellum
Operation: Blowback; automatic only
Magazine: 33-round detachable box
Sights: Blade foresight; aperture rear sight
Rate of fire: Automatic 120 rounds/min; cyclic 600 rounds/min
Effective range: 200 m
Total length: Stock extended 84 cm; stock retracted 54 cm; barrel 27.5 cm
Weight: 3.3 kg empty; 3.9 kg loaded
Manufacturer: Pabrik Sendjata Dan Mesiu
Status: No longer made but in limited service.

9mm Model VII (1957) SMG *(RSAF)*.

This is one of many 9 mm copies of the 7.62 mm Russian PPSh-41. During the latter stages of the Second World War copies of the Russian weapon were made in Iran in 7.62 mm calibre. The M22 in 9 mm was a post-war development and is still in service but is being displaced by SMG made by FN in Belgium to the Israeli Uzi design.

9 mm UZI SMG

Designed in the late 1940s this Israeli weapon incorporated features which were then major innovations but have since been widely copied. The magazine was stabilised by inserting it in the pistol grip and this permitted the easy inclusion of a grip safety. A wrap-around bolt was used in conjunction with advanced primer ignition thus making it possible to use a light bolt and to maintain a reasonable barrel length in a short total length. An ejection slot is cut in the bolt which otherwise guards against excessive back blast from the breech if a round is fired too early. The change lever has three positions, one being a safety.

Alternative fixed wooden or folding metal stocks are available and the SMG may be fitted with a bayonet or a grenade launcher.

9mm Uzi SMG with folding stock *(RMCS)*.

Ammunition: 9 mm x 19 Parabellum
Operation: Blowback; selective fire
Magazine: Detachable box with 20 or 32 rounds
Sights: Cylindrical post foresight; flip aperture rear 100/200 m
Rate of fire: Single shots 64 rounds/min; automatic 128 rounds/min; cyclic 550-600 rounds/min
Effective range: 200 m
Lengths: Fixed stock, 64 cm; folding stock extended 64 cm; stock folded 47 cm; barrel 25.5 cm
Weights: Empty 3.8 kg; loaded (25 rounds) 4.1 kg
Manufacturers: Israel Military Industries and FN Herstal
Status: In production and in service in Belgium, Iran, Israel, Netherlands, Venezuela, West Germany and elsewhere.

These two weapons are strictly obsolete in Europe and are not very likely to be found in the former Italian colonial territories. Considerable quantities of the 38/44, which was a simplified version of the 38/42, were sold to Syria, Iraq, Pakistan and Costa Rica in 1944-45, however, and it is possible that these may still be encountered. The 38/42 was an Italian Army weapon during the Second World War; and some may have been disposed of overseas.

A derivative of an earlier sequence of Beretta SMG, the 38/42 was a blowback weapon capable of selective fire using two triggers and having a fixed wooden stock of a pattern which was retained throughout the Model 38 series. It had a non-reciprocating cocking handle and a cocking way cover. The barrel of the early production models was fluted: later models had a smooth barrel and these were sometimes known as 38/43 models. All barrels were fitted with compensators.

The 38/44 simplification involved a reduction of bolt length, a change of return spring from narrow to wide diameter thus permitting the elimination of a guide rod, and simplification of the receiver end cap.

DATA (Model 38/42)
Ammunition: 9 mm Parabellum
Operation: Blowback; selective fire
Magazine: Detachable box with 20 or 40 rounds
Sights: Blade foresight; flip notch rear 100/200 m
Rate of fire: Single shots 40 rounds/min; automatic, 120 rounds/min; cyclic 550 rounds/min
Effective range: 200 m
Total length: 80 cm (barrel 21.5 cm)
Weight: 3.3 kg unloaded
Manufacturer: Beretta
Status: See text.

Production version of Beretta M38/42.

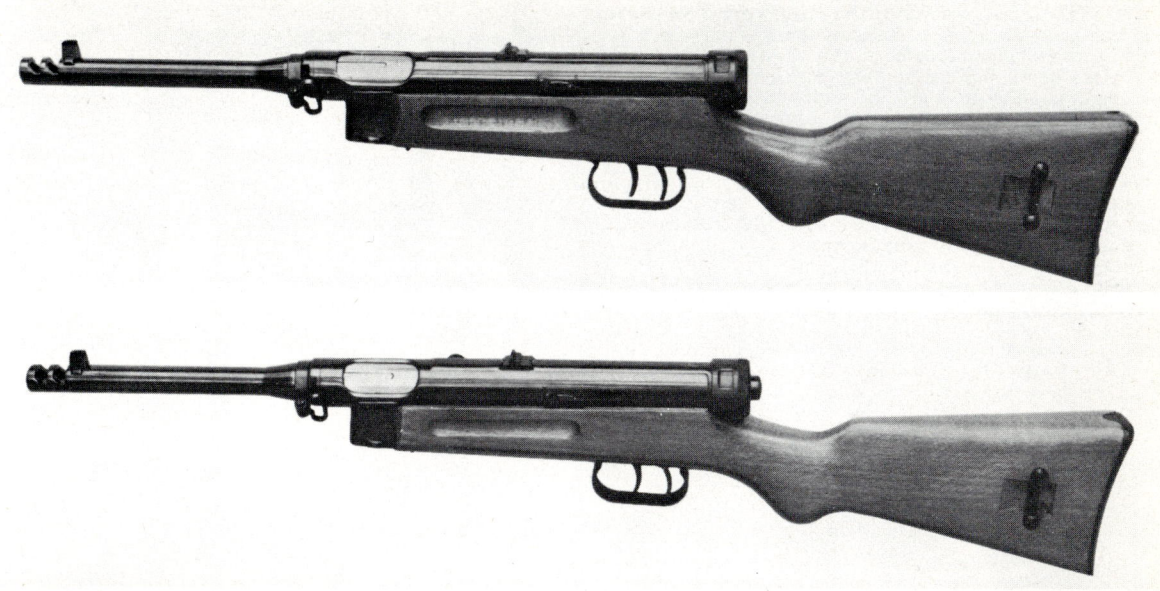

Beretta M38/43 (bottom) and M38/44.

Also known as the Model 4 this is the latest in the series of Model 38 SMG, which started before the Second World War, and has been the most successful commercially. It differs from its immediate predecessor, the 38/44, in the addition of a cross-bolt safety located above the forward trigger. It was designated Model 4 in 1958 and is still so known as the standard Italian Army weapon for general duties.

Ammunition: 9 mm Parabellum
Operation: Blowback; selective fire
Magazine: Detachable box with 20 or 40 rounds
Sights: Blade foresight; flip notch rear 100/200 m
Rate of fire: Cyclic 550 rounds/min
Total Length: 80 cm (barrel 21.5 cm)
Weight: 3.2 kg unloaded
Manufacturer: Beretta
Status: In service in Costa Rica, Dominica, Egypt (with folding bayonet), Indonesia (and copied there), Italy, Thailand, Tunis, West Germany and the Yemen.

Beretta M38/49 (Model 4) currently in service.

9 mm BERETTA MODEL 12 SMG (ITALY)

This SMG is completely different from the Model 38 range of Beretta weapons and is the final version of a series of developments between 1953 and 1959. It is used by special troops in the Italian Army — the standard weapon still being the Model 4 (M38/49) — and has been sold widely elsewhere.

Model 12 is a blowback-operated weapon capable of selective fire by change lever and having a deep wrap-around bolt. This, together with the fore-and-aft grips makes the weapon steady for full automatic fire and decreases the tendency of the muzzle to rise. There is a grip safety as well as a push-button safety. Normally fitted with a folding metal stock it can accommodate a detachable wooden stock instead.

Ammunition: 9 mm Parabellum
Operation: Blowback; selective fire
Magazine: Detachable box with 20, 30 or 40 rounds
Sights: Blade foresight; flip notch rear 100/200 m
Rate of fire: Single shots 40 rounds/min; automatic 120 rounds/min; cyclic, 550 rounds/min
Effective range: 200 m
Length: Stock extended, 64.5 cm; stock folded, 41.5 cm; barrel, 20 cm
Weight: 3.0 kg or 3.4 kg unloaded with metal or wooden stock
Manufacturer: Beretta
Status: In service in Italy. Sold to Brazil, Gabon, Libya, Nigeria, Saudi Arabia and Venezuela. Manufactured at Bandung Arsenal in Indonesia.

Beretta Model 12.

169

Two versions of this weapon have been produced. The first, known as the LF57, had a 205 mm barrel, was bought in considerable quantities by the Italian Army and is still in service. The second was a semi-automatic version with a 410 mm barrel which was exported to the USA as the Police Model 1962.

The LF57 is an automatic-only blowback weapon having several features similar to those of the Model 6 first stage of the sequence that led to the Beretta Model 12. It has a grip safety (only) and a folding stock and exhibits little tendency towards muzzle lift.

Luigi Franchi LF57 SMG.

Ammunition: 9 mm x 19 Parabellum
Operation: Blowback; automatic only
Magazine: Detachable box holding 20, 30 or 40 rounds
Sights: Blade foresight; notch rear
Rate of fire: Cyclic 450-500 rounds/min
Effective range: 200 m
Length: Stock extended, 68.5 cm; stock folded, 42.5 cm; barrel, 20.5 cm
Weight: 3.3 kg empty
Manufacturer: Luigi Franchi
Status: Made on request. Still in service in Italy and Africa.

9 mm SCK MODELS 65 AND 66 SMG

(JAPAN)

These two weapons differ only in their cyclic rates of fire: that of the M66 being only 465 rounds/min instead of 550 rounds/min. The weapons are of conventional blowback design with selective fire: special features include a grip safety on the forward magazine housing grip at the point of balance, a non-reciprocating cocking handle with a slide for the cocking way and a hinged ejection port cover which acts as a safety when closed. The barrel and barrel casing can be detached by rotating. A hinged metal stock is standard.

Ammunition: 9 mm x 19 Parabellum
Operation: Blowback; selective fire
Magazine: 30-round detachable box
Sights: Blade foresight; flip aperture rear 100/200 m
Rate of fire: Single shots 40 rounds/min; automatic 120 rounds/min; cyclic 550 rounds/min (465 rounds/min for M66)
Effective range: 200 m
Lengths: Stock extended, 76 cm; stock folded, 50 cm
Manufacturer: Shin Chuo Kogyo
Status: In production and in Japanese Army service.

SCK 9mm Model 65 SMG.

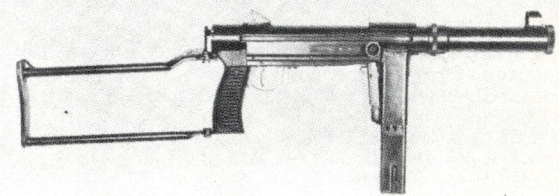

SCK Model 66.

(LUXEMBOURG)

Two models of this weapon were produced by the Sociétè Luxembourgeoise d'Armes in the mid 1950s. Neither was very successful and both failed to capture a European market. A few were sold in North Africa and South America, however, and may still be encountered.

The two models are known as the 'Super' and the 'Light'. Both are designed for cheapness and production simplicity and the 'Light' model was introduced to add a weight reduction to the sales appeal. Both are conventional blowback weapons with selective fire capability and adjustable telescopic stocks, and the 'Super' has a muzzle brake and compensator and an ejection port cover.

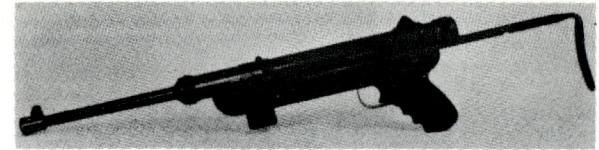

9mm Sola Model Super *(RSAF)*.

Ammunition: 9 mm x 19 Parabellum
Operation: Blowback; selective fire
Magazine: 32-round detachable box
Sights: Blade foresight; flip aperture 50/150 m and 100 m notch rear
Rate of fire: Cyclic 550 rounds/min
Effective range: 150 m
Length: Stock extended 89 cm (Light — 78.5 cm); stock retracted 61 cm (57 cm); barrel 30.5 cm (20.5 cm)
Weight: Unloaded 2.9 kg (2.7 kg); loaded 3.6 kg (3.4 kg)
Manufacturer: Sociétè Luxembourgeoise d'Armes
Status: Not now made. Possibly exists in North Africa or South America.

172

9 mm MODEL HM-3 SMG

(MEXICO)

This SMG is a light weapon in which the length has been kept down by using an extensive wrap-around of the bolt. It is blowback operated with selective fire and has a fixed metal stock and a grip safety on the combined magazine housing and pistol grip.

Ammunition: 9 mm x 19 Parabellum
Operation: Blowback; selective fire
Magazine: 32-round detachable box
Rate of fire: Cyclic, 600 rounds/min
Total length: 63.5 cm (barrel 25.5 cm)
Weight: Empty 3.0 kg; loaded 3.4 kg
Manufacturer: Productos Mendoza
Status: Production.

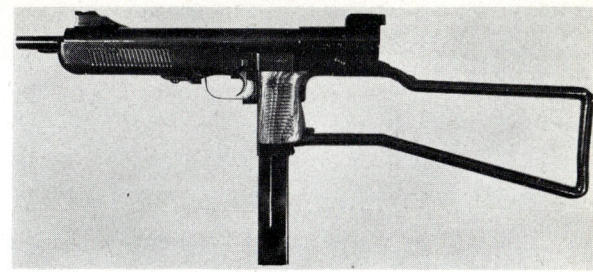

Productos Mendoza HM-3 SMG.

This weapon was designed in Portugal but incorporates features of German and US SMG. It is a conventional blowback device, offering automatic fire only, and its least conventional feature is the provision for attaching a bayonet. It has a retracting wire stock similar to that of the US M3.

Ammunition: 9 mm x 19 Parabellum
Operation: Blowback; automatic only
Magazine: 32-round detachable box
Sights: Blade foresight; fixed aperture rear 100 m
Rate of fire: Cyclic 500 rounds/min
Effective range: 100 m
Lengths: Stock extended 81.5 cm; stock retracted 63.5 cm; barrel 25 cm
Weight: 3.7 kg empty; 4.4 kg loaded
Manufacturer: Fabrica de Braco de Prato
Status: No longer made. In service with Portuguese forces and probably now to be found in former Portuguese colonies.

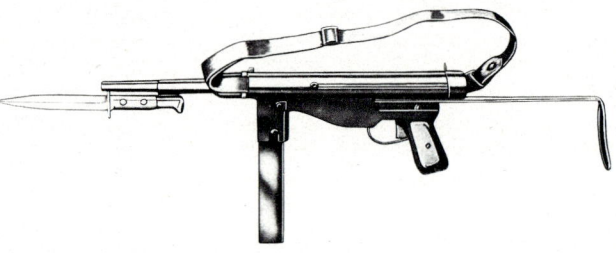

Portuguese 9mm M48 *(J. Smith)*.

9 mm ORITA M1941 SMG (ROMANIA)

This is an elderly weapon which was made in 1941-44 and has long since been withdrawn from first-line service. It still survives, however, in People's Militia and police units. In appearance it resembles the German MP40 but is a more robust and well-made weapon. Most have wooden butts and straight magazines; but metal stocks and curved magazines may be encountered. Operation is simple blowback with selective fire; but, as in the early Thompson, the hammer, carried in the bolt head, is rotated to fire by a projection in the bolt way.

9mm Orita M1941.

Ammunition: 9 mm Parabellum
Operation: Blowback; selective fire
Magazine: 25-round straight or 32-round curved box
Sights: Blade foresight; tangent rear notch 100-500 m
Rate of fire: Single shots, 40 rounds/min; automatic, 120 rounds/min; cyclic, 600 rounds/min
Effective range: 200 m
Total length: 89.5 cm (barrel 28.5 cm)
Weight: 3.5 kg empty. 4.0 kg loaded
Manufacturer: Cugir Arsenal
Status: No longer made. In service with People's Militia and police units.

Based on the German MP40, this weapon differs in having the cocking handle on the right, a perforated barrel jacket and a barrel which can be easily removed by unscrewing. It is blowback-operated with selective fire capability and has a muzzle compensator. Safety has been improved by the addition of a catch to the cocking handle which secures the bolt in the forward position. Like the MP40 it has a folding metal stock.

Ammunition: 9 mm Largo
Operation: Blowback; selective fire by trigger pressure
Magazine: 30-round detachable box
Sights: Blade foresight; flip notch rear 100/200 m
Rate of fire: Cyclic 450 rounds/min
Effective range: 200 m
Lengths: Stock open, 84 cm; stock folded 58 cm; barrel 20 cm
Weight: 3.9 kg empty; 4.5 kg loaded
Manufacturer: Bonifacio Echeverria
Status: No longer made. In service in Spanish Army. Sold to Chile, Cuba, Portugal and Saudi Arabia, all in small quantities. Being replaced in Spanish service by Z62.

9 mm STAR MODEL Z62 SMG   (SPAIN)

This is a conventional blowback weapon which is replacing the Z45 in Spanish Army service. Significant features include the addition of a bolt inertia safety behind the spring-loaded firing pin which, independently of any action on the part of the firer, prevents accidental discharge by dropping. Selective fire is obtained by operating the lower portion of the trigger for single shots and the upper portion for automatic. There is a push-through safety in the upper part of the pistol grip. The folding stock is similar to that of the Czech Vz25. The weapon is made in both 9 mm Largo (as was the Z45) and 9 mm Parabellum.

9mm Star Model Z-62.

Ammunition: 9 mm Largo or Parabellum
Operation: Blowback; selective fire
Magazine: Detachable box with 20, 30 or 40 rounds
Sights: Blade foresight; flip aperture rear 100/200 m
Rate of fire: Cyclic 550 rounds/min
Effective range: 200 m
Lengths: Stock extended, 70 cm; stock folded, 48 cm; barrel 20 cm
Weight: 2.9 kg empty, 3.5 kg loaded with 30 rounds
Manufacturer: Bonifacio Echeverria
Status: In production and in service with Spanish forces.

This weapon was introduced into Spanish Army service in 1971. It is in most respects identical with the earlier Z62 but was introduced because of difficulties with the selective fire trigger mechanism. In the Z70B the trigger selection arrangement has been replaced by a conventional trigger and a selector on the left of the receiver above the pistol grip and the push-through safety has been replaced by a catch under the trigger guard.

All other characteristics are the same as for the Z62.

Star Model Z-70B.

9 mm PORT SAID SMG   (UNITED ARAB REPUBLIC)

This is close copy of the Swedish Carl Gustav which has been made in fairly substantial numbers in Egypt. Performance is believed to be substantially the same as that of the original weapon; and the SMG is in sevice with Egyptian forces, and was used in the 1973 war, although the standard weapons for first-line troops are the Russian AK47 and AKM rifles.

The 'Port Said' copy of the Carl Gustav *(RSAF)*.

Widely known simply as the Carl Gustav this weapon was originally made (as the M45) to use the Suomi 50-round box magazine which had been used in the earlier M37-39 weapon. In 1948, however, Carl Gustav developed a highly reliable two-column magazine holding 36 rounds which has since been adopted and copied in several other countries. To enable this to be used with the M45 a detachable housing was developed which would permit the use of either magazine, and weapons with this housing were designated M45B. Since 1951, however, the gun has been made with the housing permanently fixed so that it will accept only the 36-round magazine which is now the standard item. Earlier versions still survive, however, especially in overseas service.

Apart from this complication the gun is of conventional blowback design, firing automatically, and is fitted with a folding metal stock. A special silenced version was designed for the American CIA and saw some service with special forces in Vietnam.

Carl Gustav M45 with silencer *(RSAF)*.

Ammunition: 9 mm Parabellum
Operation: Blowback; Automatic only
Magazine: 40-round Suomi or 36-round Carl Gustav (see text)
Sights: Protected post foresight; flip rear 100/200 m
Rate of fire: Cyclic 550-600 rounds/min
Effective range: 200 m
Lengths: Stock extended, 81 cm; stock folded, 55 cm; barrel 18 cm
Weight: 3.4 kg empty; 4.2 kg loaded with 36 rounds
Manufacturer: Carl Gustav
Status: No longer manufactured. Still in service with Swedish forces. Supplied also to Egypt and Indonesia (and copied in both countries).

Current model of the M45.

One of the best-known of all SMG the Sten was designed in 1940 and demonstrated and put into production in 1941, whereafter some four million of various models were made before the end of the Second World War. Of these the commonest were the Mk II and the Mk III; but the other marks differed mainly in such details as the design of the stock and the presence or absence of a pistol grip, foregrip, bayonet fitting and so forth. The official marks ran from I to VI with three duplications but the interchangeability of most parts increased the number of possible variations beyond this. In terms of quality the best version was the Mk V — one of the best SMG of the war — which had a wooden butt and an improved trigger and grip configuration.

A simple blowback weapon with a heavy bolt and fixed firing pin, the Sten was designed for cheapness of production, and the only basic feature that can be said to involve a departure from this concept was the provision for

9mm Sten Mk I* *(RMCS)*.

Sten Mk II *(RMCS)*.

Silenced Sten MkIIS *(RMCS)*.

selective fire by a push-button change device. No applied safety was provided: when cocked the cocking handle was rotated into a slot cut above the cocking way; alternatively the gun could be carried with the bolt closed on an empty breech. In the latter state, however, there was a danger that if the gun were dropped on its butt the bolt would set back far enough to chamber a round and fire it; and in later models the cocking handle could be pressed through to lock the bolt in the forward position.

A weakness of all Sten models was the poorly-designed magazine. Its lips were easily damaged or deformed enough to prevent the rounds from feeding properly, it was easily clogged with dirt and, being a single column device, it could effectively be loaded only with a filler tool.

A silenced version of the Mk II, called the Mk II S, was one of the best silenced SMG made during the war. The Mk VI was a silenced version of the Mk V.

Ammunition: 9 mm Parabellum
Operation: Blowback; selective fire
Magazine: 32-round-detachable box
Sights: Blade foresight; aperture rear
Rate of fire: Single shots, 40 rounds/min; automatic 128 rounds/min; cyclic 540 rounds/min (Mks I — III), 575 rounds/min (Mks IV — VI)
Effective range: 200 m, but 150 m for the silenced models
Lengths: Mks II, III and V 76 cm; Mks II S and VI 85.5 cm; barrel, Mks II, III and V 20 cm
Weights: Empty, Mk II 2.8 kg; Mk III 3.2 kg; Mk V 3.9 kg; Mk II S 3.5 kg; Mk VI 4.3 kg
Manufacturers: BSA and ROF. Also made by Long Branch Arsenal in Canada
Status: No longer made or in service in any European or North American army, but likely to be encountered almost anywhere in the world.

Mk V Standard model *(RMCS).*

Sten Mk VI *(RSAF).*

(UK)

9 mm (STERLING) L2A3 SMG

This is the current British Army SMG and is the military version of the Sterling Mk 4. The design was originally that of G.W. Patchett in 1942 and it was produced by Sterling in 1944 and then in modified form until 1954. This, the Sterling Mk 3, was adopted as the L2A1 by the British Army in 1953 and a slightly modified version came into service as the L2A2 in 1955. The L2A3 entered service in 1956.

The Sterling is a blowback weapon and has a cylindrical bolt with a fixed firing pin and extractor claw. As a round, stripped from the side-mounted magazine, aligns itself with the bore the extractor grips its base; and chamber friction causes the firing pin to detonate the primer before the round is fully home. This advanced primer ignition permits the use of a relatively light bolt.

The gun has a selective fire lever which incorporates a safety position. A 34-round magazine is standard, but the gun will also accept Sten, Lanchester or Canadian C1 magazines. A simple folding metal stock is fitted.

9mm L2A3 SMG *(RMCS)*.

Ammunition: 9 mm x 19 Parabellum
Operation: Blowback; selective fire
Magazine: 34-round box (see text)
Sights: Blade foresight; flip aperture rear 100/200 yards.
Rate of fire: Single shots 40 rounds/min; automatic 102 rounds/min; cyclic 550 rounds/min
Effective range: 200 m
Length: Stock extended, 71 cm; stock folded, 48.5 cm; barrel 20 cm
Weight: Empty 3.0 kg; loaded 3.5 kg
Date introduced: 1956 (L2A3)
Manufacturer: Sterling and RSAF
Status: In service with British, Canadian, New Zealand and other forces. Some 78 countries have purchased the Sterling Mk 4 in various quantities: the larger buyers are India (where the gun is now made under licence), Malaysia, Tunisia and Ghana. Considerable quantities have also been sold to Nigeria and Libya.

Sterling Mk 4.

This is the silenced version of the L2A3 SMG used by the British Army. There is a commercial version which is known as the Patchett/Sterling Mk V.

Silencing is achieved by using a barrel with 72 radial holes drilled in it to permit propellant gas to escape into a diffuser tube which is perforated and surrounded by an expanded metal wrap within the outer barrel casing. This casing extends beyond the muzzle and in this position there is a helical diffuser which imparts a swirling action to the gases following the bullet as it and they pass through the centre of the diffuser. The effect of all these measures is to reduce the velocity of both the bullet and such gases as finally emerge from the casing below the speed of sound in air.

As these measures reduce the effective blowback pressure a lighter bolt has to be used for the mechanism to work.

Characteristics are generally similar to the L2A3 but the addition of the silencer and other changes increases the weight of the weapon by about 0.9 kg and the length by some 17.5 cm. The cyclic rate of fire is slightly lower and the effective range is reduced to 150 m.

Manufacturer: Sterling
Status: In production and in British Army service.

9mm Patchett/Sterling Mk 5.

9 mm ATCHISSON M1957 SMMG

This is one of several SMG developed as private ventures by Maxwell Atchisson in the USA and marketed by Defence Systems International. It is a light, compact blowback weapon with a combined magazine housing and grip behind the trigger guard and a small wooden foregrip immediately in front of the guard. A steel wire stock, similar to that of the M3, is fitted. There is no cocking handle.

Ammunition: 9 mm x 19 Parabellum
Operation: Blowback; selective fire
Magazine: 32-round detachable box
Sights: Blade foresight; aperture rear
Effective range: 200 m
Length: Stock extended, 61 cm; stock retracted, 38.5 cm; barrel 20.5 cm
Weight: 2.1 kg empty
Manufacturer: WAK
Status: Available.

Atchisson 9mm M1957 SMG *(Bintliff)*.

9 mm M3 SMG

As noted in the entry for the standard 0.45 in M3 SMG, a 9 mm conversion was produced in 1944 for the US Office of Strategic Studies. The conversion involved the provision of a magazine adaptor, a new barrel and bolt and a single-column magazine of the Sten type.

About 25,000 converted weapons were made in 1944 for use in the South Pacific war zone and some may still survive. Apart from the changes noted above the characteristics of the weapon are broadly similar to those given for the 0.45 in M3.

This is one of two SMG models developed after George Ingram joined the Sionics firm in Atlanta in 1969, a partnership which led to the formation of the Military Armament Corporation (MAC) in 1970.

The basic design is a very short blowback-operated SMG using a wrap-around bolt to save space behind the breech and having a combined pistol grip and magazine housing and an optional retractable stock. Provision is made for selective fire, the change lever being separate from the safety catch: and as an additional safety measure the bolt may be locked by twisting the cocking handle through a right-angle. This handle is mounted on top of the receiver and has a U-notch cut in it to leave a clear sight path: the firer is thus warned that the bolt is unlocked by the sight obstruction caused by rotating the handle.

Both the Model 10 and the similar Model 11 have muzzles externally threaded to take the MAC suppressor. This differs from most silencers in that it does not slow the bullet below sonic speed but uses a system of conflicting gas streams to slow the emergent gases to subsonic levels. The 'crack' of the bullet thus remains but the more easily located 'thump' from the gun is eliminated.

The Model 10 is available in both 9 mm Parabellum and 0.45 ACP: the Model 11 is chambered for the 9 mm Short (.380 ACP). Data are given below for the 9 mm Model 10: data for other calibres are separately entered. All three are notable for the high cyclic rate of fire.

Ammunition: 9 mm Parabellum
Operation: Blowback; selective fire
Magazine: 32-round box
Sights: Blade foresight; aperture rear set for 100 m
Rate of fire: Single shots, 40 rounds/min; automatic, 96 rounds/min; cyclic, 1090 rounds/min
Effective range: 100 m
Lengths: Stock extended, 55 cm; stock retracted, 27 cm; no stock, 26.5 cm; barrel 14.5 cm; extra for suppressor, 25 cm
Weight: Empty 2.8 kg; loaded 3.5 kg; suppressor 0.5 kg
Manufacturer: MAC
Status: With other M 10 versions and M 11, sold to Chile, Colombia, Dominican Republic, Saudi Arabia, UK, USA and Yugoslavia. Quantities in some instances are believed to be small.

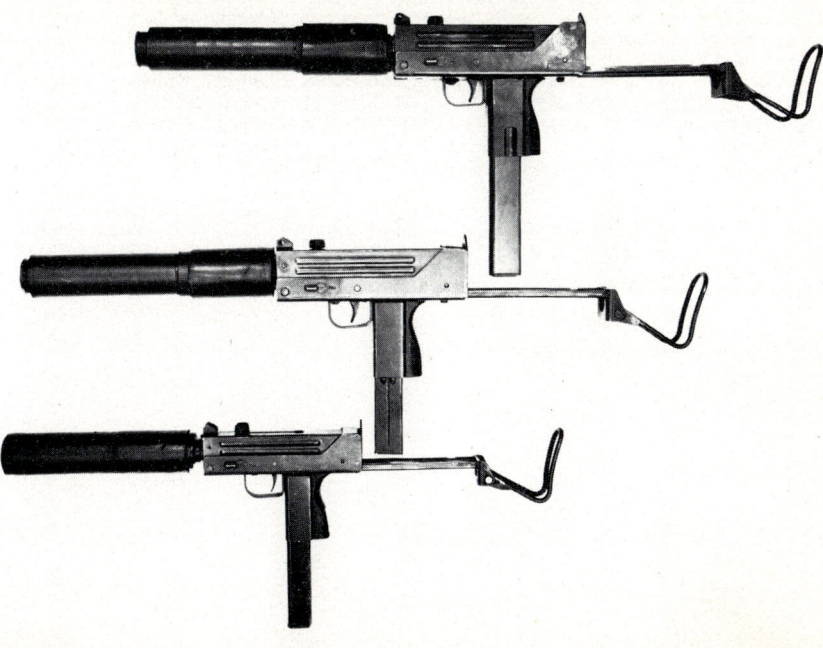

Ingram M10 and M11 SMG *(RMCS)*.

This model of the Ingram SMG is chambered for the 9 mm Short (.380 ACP) round and is a smaller weapon than the Model 10. In design and operation it is similar, however, and the general description of both the weapon and the suppressor given in the Model 10 entry is equally applicable to the Model 11. Physical and performance data differ in many particulars, however, and these differences are summarised below.

Ammunition: 9 mm Short (.380 ACP)
Magazine: Box holding 16 or 32 rounds
Sights: Blade foresight; aperture rear set for 50 m
Rate of fire: Cyclic, 1,200 rounds/min
Length: Stock extended 46 cm; stock retracted 25 cm; no stock 22 cm; barrel, 13 cm; extra for suppressor, 19 cm
Weight: Empty 1.6 kg; loaded 1.9 kg (16) or 2.1 kg (32); extra for suppressor 0.5 kg

9 mm FOOTE MP970 SMG

(USA)

This is a compact blowback automatic weapon using a bolt with a fixed firing pin and requiring only simple manufacturing techniques for its construction. It can be handled with or without a stock.

Ammunition: 9 mm x 19 Parabellum
Operation: Blowback; automatic only
Magazine: 32-round detachable box
Sights: Blade foresight; notch rear
Rate of fire: Cyclic, 650 rounds/min
Effective range: 200 m
Length: With stock, 62 cm; without stock, 38 cm; barrel 20.5 cm
Weight: Empty, 3.0 kg
Status: Designed by John P. Foote. Prototype stage.

Foote MP970 SMG *(D. Thomas)*.

This weapon combines some characteristics of an SMG with some of those of a rifle. It uses a basic Ingram SMG body but adds a carbine-length barrel and offers options of telescopic metal or fixed wooden stocks, the whole being convertible to the original SMG configuration. As with the Ingram Model 10 on which it is based alternatives chambered for 9 mm Parabellum or 0.45 ACP are contemplated. The following data relate to the 9 mm version.

Ammunition: 9 mm Parabellum
Operation: Blowback; selective fire
Magazine: 32-round detachable box
Sights: Hooded post foresight; adjustable rear 50-350 m
Rate of fire: Cyclic 1,090 rounds/min
Lengths: Stock extended 83 cm; stock retracted 64 cm; barrel 45 cm
Weight: Empty 3.6 kg; loaded 4.3 kg
Manufacturer: MAC
Status: Prototype stage.

9mm LR Assault SMG.

0.45-in HALCON SMG

Between 1943 and the early 1960s the arms factory of Halcon at Buenos Aires produced four different types of blowback-operated SMG all chambered primarily for the .45ACP cartridge.

These weapons are now obsolete and current SMG in Argentina all use the 9 mm Parabellum round. A few of the earlier weapons may have found their way into irregular forces in Latin America but it is unlikely.

Halcon M1943 SMG.

Halcon Model 1946.

Halcon Light Model 60.

(BRAZIL)

0.45-in MB50 AND INA 953 SMG

These two weapons are almost identical. The MB50 is a 0.45 licence-built copy of the Danish 9 mm Madsen Model 1946 with Brazilian markings (a crest on the left of the receiver and the words "Exercito Brasiliero"). The 953 has an enlarged magazine housing and the cocking handle is on the right of the receiver instead of at the top.

Ammunition: .45 ACP
Operation: Blowback; automatic only
Magazine: 30-round box
Sights: Blade foresight; 100 m aperture rear
Rate of fire: Cyclic 650 rounds/min
Effective range: 200 m
Total length: Stock extended, 79.5 cm; stock retracted, 54.5 cm; barrel 21.5 cm
Manufacturer: INA
Status: No longer in production. In reserve service in Brazil and probably elsewhere in South America.

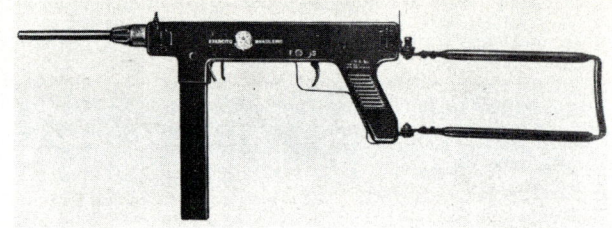

INA MB50 SMG.

0.45-in TYPE 36 SMG

This is a Chinese (Nationalist) copy of the US wartime M3A1 SMG — the designation 36 indicating that it was made in 1947 since the Chinese Nationalist calendar started in 1911. Details of the weapon can be found in the corresponding American entry. The Type 36 is still in first-line service in Taiwan: its American equivalent is also still in service there and in other parts of Asia including mainland China.

A version of the Type 36 made to use the 9 mm Parabellum round has a separate entry. Both this (Type 37) and the Type 36 have Chinese markings stamped on the left side of the magazine housing, and although their component parts are in general interchangeable with those of the M3A1 the finish is poorer.

11 mm (0.45-in) ball ammunition for the Type 36 is made in Taiwan but US .45-in M1911 pistol ball ammunition can also be fired.

A version of the US Thompson SMG was made in Egypt during the 1950s. Barrels and magazines were imported from the USA and some modifications were introduced. The cocking handle was moved from the top to the side of the receiver, a new rear sight was fitted and there was a screw-on end cap for the receiver. In other respects the weapon, of which only a small quantity was made, is similar to the standard Thompson.

Egyptian-made Thompson SMG.

0.45-in THOMPSON SMG

(USA)

This famous weapon originated in a design created during the First World War and became famous in the gang warfare in the 1920s. Various models were produced, but the important ones are the pre-war M1928A1 and the Second World War models M1 and M1A1. There were various mechanical differences between these three, but the significant ones are set out below.

Thompson Model 1928 A1 *(RMCS)*.

M1928A1: Adjustable leaf rear sight. Radial-finned barrel with compensator. Blish H-piece blowback delay device and top-mounted actuator knob for cocking. Firing pin operated by hammer rotated by post in bolt way.
M1: Simple aperture sight. Plain barrel and no compensator. No Blish mechanism and actuator replaced by simple side cocking handle. Firing pin and hammer as above.
M1A1: As M1 but fixed firing pin and no hammer.

Common characteristics include a selective fire change lever and separate safety, a wooden stock (removable on the M1928A1) and a choice of magazines. Some 1,400,000 Thompson SMG of various types were made — not counting copies made in Vietnam — and their use is still widespread, largely as a result of their distribution under US military aid programmes.

Model M1 Thompson SMG *(RMCS)*.

(USA)

Ammunition: 0.45ACP
Operation: Blowback (with delay in M1928A1); selective fire
Magazine: Box with 20 or 30 rounds or drum with 50 or 100 rounds
Sights: Blade foresight; 0-600 yd leaf aperture rear (M1928A1) or fixed aperture and V-notch
Rate of fire: Single shots 40 rounds/min; automatic 120 rounds/min; cyclic 700 rounds/min
Effective range: 200 m (maximum range about 1500 m)
Total length: 85 cm (M1928A1) or 81 cm; barrel, 26.5 cm; M1928A1 without butt, 63.5 cm
Weight: Empty gun only 4.9 kg (M1928A1) or 4.8 kg; empty magazines from 0.2 kg to 1.8 kg; loaded magazines from 0.6 kg to 3.9 kg
Manufacturers: Auto Ordnance Corporation. Savage Arms Co
Status: No longer in production. Still found in Ireland, South-East Asia (some locally made), possibly Egypt (locally made) and elsewhere. Chinese copies of the early 1921 model may also occasionally be encountered.

The M1A1 model of the Thompson SMG *(RMCS)*.

0.45-in M3 SMG

(USA)

This weapon was designed to satisfy a wartime need for a cheaper US SMG than the Thompson. After a few preliminary designs it was adopted late in 1942 by the US Army as the M3 and over 600,000 were made. It is a simple blowback weapon giving automatic fire only. Two features that have been copied elsewhere are the telescopic stock and the safety lock associated with the ejection port cover which prevents the weapon from being fired when the port is closed. A rather complicated, and subsequently troublesome, lever and pawl cocking mechanism is mounted on the right of the receiver (see the entry for the M3A1).

A silenced version of the weapon was developed for the Office of Strategic Services in 1944 but only about 1000 were made. A 9 mm version was also made in larger quantity for the same customer. For general use a flash hider was developed for optional addition to the gun.

0.45 M3 SMG *(RMCS)*.

Ammunition: .45ACP
Operation: Blowback; automatic only
Magazine: 30-round detachable box
Sights: Blade foresight; aperture rear set for 100 yards
Rate of fire: Cyclic, 450 rounds/min
Effective range: 200 m
Lengths: Stock extended, 75.5 cm; stock retracted, 58 cm; barrel 20.5 cm
Weight: Empty 4.1 kg; loaded, 4.7 kg
Date introduced: 1942
Manufacturer: General Motors

Status: No longer manufactured or in regular US service. Together with the M3A1 it is used by several South American countries and may be encountered among insurgent forces almost anywhere.

As noted in the entry for the M3 weapon of the same calibre, the lever and pawl cocking mechanism used in that SMG was troublesome. In 1944, investigation showed that the mechanism was not really necessary and that an adequate cocking arrangement could be made by making a finger cavity in the bolt so that the soldier could cock the weapon with his forefinger. This modification was introduced and the lever and pawl removed: at the same time some other small alterations were made, including a larger ejection port, a redesigned barrel ratchet and the addition of a guard over the magazine catch and of a magazine filler and stock plate to the stock. All these changes reduced manufacturing costs.

This modified design was adopted as the M3A1 and some 50,000 were made between 1945 and the end of the Korean war. Characteristics of the M3A1 are generally similar to those of the M3 except for a reduction of about 0.2 kg in weight. The notes on the manufacture and status of the M3 are also applicable to the M3A1 except that the production for the Korean war was undertaken by the Ithaca Gun Co. and that a copy of the M3A1 was made in Communist China and is separately described.

M3A1 SMG *(RMCS)*.

0.45-in INGRAM MODELS 6 AND 7 SMG

These two weapons were developed as part of the early series of SMG for which Gordon Ingram was responsible before his association with MAC led to the M10 and M11 developments. Models 6 and 7 were the only members of this early series to have been made in sufficient quantity for it to be likely that they will still be encountered. About 15,000 were sold in North America and a further 8,000 to Peru. Both models are conventional blowback weapons with wooden stocks: apart from different foregrips the main difference between them is that the M7 fires from the closed bolt position.

Manufacturer: Police Ordnance Company
Status: Probably still to be found in South America.

Ingram Model 6 (bottom) and Model 7 *(Ingram)*.

General details of the Ingram Model 10 SMG are given in the entry for the 9 mm version. The following data relate to the 0.45 ACP version and are restricted to those items that are different for the two versions.

Ammunition: 0.45ACP
Magazine: 30-round detachable box
Rate of fire: Automatic, 90 rounds/min; cyclic 1,145 rounds/min
Weight: Loaded 3.8 kg.

0.45-in LR ASSAULT SMG

This weapon, based on the Ingram Model 10, is described in the corresponding 9 mm entry. The following data distinguish the 0.45ACP version from the 9 mm Parabellum weapon.

Ammunition: 0.45ACP
Magazine: 30-round detachable box
Rate of fire: Cyclic 1,145 rounds/min
Weight: Loaded 4.7 kg

0.45-in VIET CONG THOMPSON SMG

Among many weapons copied by the Vietnamese during the war in their country was the Thompson SMG. Simplified versions resembling the M1A1 were encountered in Viet Cong hands. Some of these copies may still be in service.

Vietnamese copy of the Thompson SMG *(VSMC)*.

WEAPON MANUFACTURE

INTRODUCTION

This section is intended to be read in conjunction with the preceding weapon sections. It provides some supplementary information concerning the manufacturers whose products are described in the earlier sections, together with a little information on manufacturers whose obsolete products are not included in the main body of the book.

No attempt has been made to deal with countries such as the USSR or the People's Republic of China because so little information on their individual manufacturing organisations is available. Countries such as Czechoslovakia are included, however, because weapons made by identifiable manufacturers are still to be found.

An (alphabetical) arrangement by countries has been adopted because it may help to convey an impression of the extent and significance of weapon development and manufacture in each country.

Before the First World War the Army used a Mannlicher pistol manufactured at Steyr in Austria. In 1916 this was replaced by a copy of the Colt 1911 made at the Fabrica Militar de Armas Portatilas (an ordnance factory) at Rosario, Santa Fe. Most of the Mannlichers were sold to the USA. A later copy, the M1927, was also made at Rosario; and the current army weapon, a licence-built copy of the FN Browning HP, comes from the same factory.

A simplified copy of the Colt 1911 was the Ballester Molina made by HAFDASA— Hispano Argentina Fabrica de Automoviles SA — of Buenos Aires. The weapon is still in service but HAFDASA no longer make arms.

Several sub-machine guns were made during and after the Second World War by the arms factory of Halcon at Buenos Aires. More recently a new (PA) series, including the PA3 currently in service, has been made at the Rosario ordnance factory.

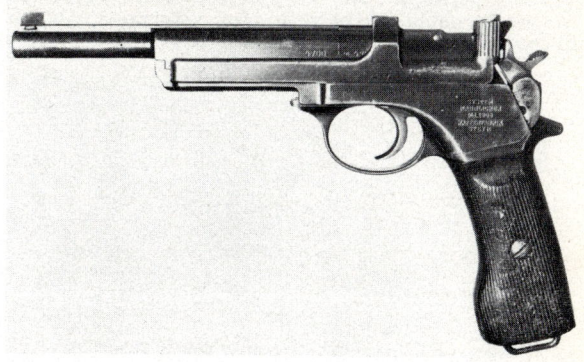

Argentinian (Mannlicher) 7.65mm M1905 *(RSAF)*.

AUSTRALIA

During the Second World War the Austen SMG was made by Diecasters Ltd. and by W.J. Carmichael and Co. both of Melbourne. Its successor, the Owen SMG, was made by Lysaght Newcastle Works, Newcastle, N.S.W. The F1 SMG currently in service was made by the Small Arms Factory at Lithgow, N.S.W.

Prior to the First World War the Austrian Army was equipped with pistols made at the Osterreichische Waffenfabrik at Steyr and by Femaru Fegyver in Budapest. Steyr pistols have continued in use since then and the current weapon is the Walther P38 manufactured by Steyr-Daimler-Puch.

Between the wars a joint venture between Steyr-Daimler-Puch and Solothum in Switzerland produced one of the earlier SMG, the Steyr-Solothum M1930; and after the second war the Austrian firm recommenced independent design and now produces the MPi 69 SMG.

One of the most recent of the SMG developments described in the weapon sections is the 0.22 in AM 180 weapon made by Voere GmbH at Kufstein.

9mm MP34 SMG (Steyr-Solothum).

BELGIUM

In Belgium the association between John Browning and the national ordnance factory now known simply as FN. Herstal, Liège, has produced some of the world's best-known pistols starting with the M1900 and continuing to the HP pistol which is still in production at Herstal and elsewhere.

Belgium's first SMG was the M34 made by Anciens Etablissements Pieper at Herstal and was a copy of the German MP28. Currently in service, however, though no longer in production is the Mitraillette Vigneron M2 made by SA Précision Liègeoise, Herstal. The Israeli Uzi is currently in production at FN for export.

9mm Browning M1903.

Pieper 9mm M34 SMG.

BRAZIL

A copy of the Danish Madsen M1948 SMG was made by Industria National de Armas SA, Sao Paulo. Known as the INA .45 SMG it is still in service with reserve units but no longer in production.

CANADA

John Inglis and Co., of Toronto, made the FN Browning HP pistol during the Second World War. Production was originally set up to supply the Chinese forces fighting against the Japanese; but the weapons were also issued to British airborne and commando units. Since the war a later version (No 2 Mk 1*) of the pistol has been issued to Australian, British and Canadian forces; and spares for this weapon are still made by Canadian Arsenals Ltd., Long Branch, Ontario. In 1950 the North American Arms Co., Toronto, produced a modification of the Browning HP called the NAACO Brigadier, but it did not go into production.

During the Second World War the Long Branch factory made large quantities of the Sten SMG. More recently a modified version of the British L2A1 SMG was made by Canadian Arsenals Ltd., It is known as the C1 and is in service with Canadian forces but is no longer made.

CHINA (TAIWAN)

A small-arms industry was set up with American help not long after the Chinese Nationalists retreated to Formosa. Among its products have been copies of the US M3A1 SMG made in both 0.45 and 9 mm calibres.

CZECHOSLOVAKIA

Between the wars and until the country came wholly under Russian control, a range of pistols was made by Ceskoslovenska Zbrojovka, Strakonice, the last one positively in the sequence being the M50. The M52 was made at the Uherskybrod Ordnance Factory and the Vz61 Skorpion is believed to have been made by Ceskoslovenska Zbrojovka.

Also made by Zbrojovka at the Brno plant were the ZK383, 466 and 467 between-wars SMG and the post-war Vz 23, 24, 25 and 26 weapons.

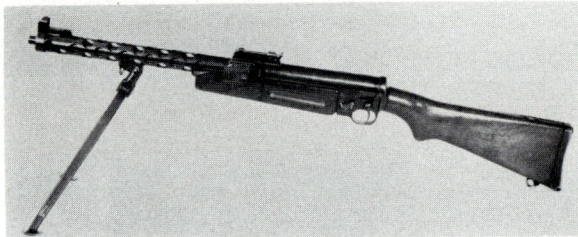

9mm ZK 383 SMG *(RSAF)*.

Before the First World War the Danish Army adopted the Belgian M1910 pistol made by Anciens Establissements Pieper at Herstal. After the war a slight variant of this weapon was put into production in Denmark and was made by Haerens Tojhus København. In 1940 the FN Browning HP was adopted and in 1948 the Swiss SIG 210-2 which is the current weapon. It, the FN Browning and some Swedish Lahti pistols have all been imported.

Post-war sub-machine guns, however, have been made in Denmark by Dansk Industri Syndikat, Madsen, København and their series of weapons has been widely adopted and copied.

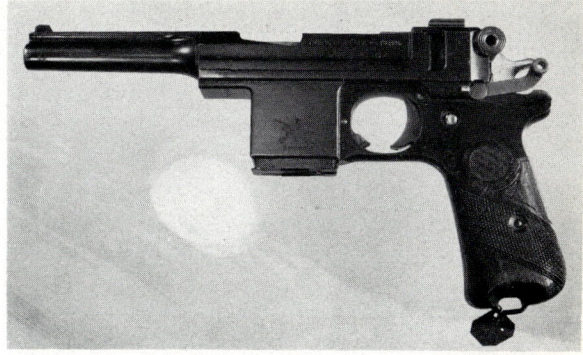

9mm Model 1910 pistol made by Pieper.

DOMINICAN REPUBLIC

Pistols for the Dominican Army are imported from the USA (Colt and Smith and Wesson) and from Belgium (FN Browning HP). The arsenal set up at San Cristobal in 1948, however, makes a delayed blowback sub-machine carbine, the M2, which is in service with Dominican forces and some of which have been sold to Cuba.

FINLAND

Until 1935 Finnish forces used the Luger; but after that they adopted the M35 Lahti pistol. This is made by Valtion Kiväärithedas (VKT) at Jyväskylä and is also made in slightly modified form in Sweden.

Finland was a European leader in SMG design after the First World War and produced a series of weapons from 1922 onwards. The most successful of this series of 'Suomi' designs was the M31, which was also made in Sweden by Husqvarna and by Hispano Suiza in Switzerland and was sold to Norway. The current Finnish SMG is a copy of the Russian PPS-43 and both it and the M31 were made by Oy Tikkakoski Ab, Sakara.

French arms manufacturers have a long history of pistol manufacture. Probably the earliest which might still be encountered outside a collection is the 1892 Lebel revolver, but self-loading pistols made between the wars are still in widespread use. Post-war weapons still in service with the French Army include the MAS M1950 which is made by the ordnance factories at Chatellerault and St. Etienne and the MAB P15 made by Manufacture d'Armes Automatiques, Bayonne and still in production.

Licenced manufacture of the German Walther pistol is carried out by Manufacture de Machines du Haut-Rhin (Manurhin), Mulhouse-Bourtzwiller.

A sub-machine gun, the MAS M38, was made before the Second World War at St. Etienne. The current weapon is the MAT49, made by Manufacture d'Armes de Tulle, but it is no longer in production. A recent development, now in production but of uncertain military status, is the 9 mm SMG made by Gevarm and Gevelot, Paris.

8mm Model 1892 revolver *(RSAF)*.

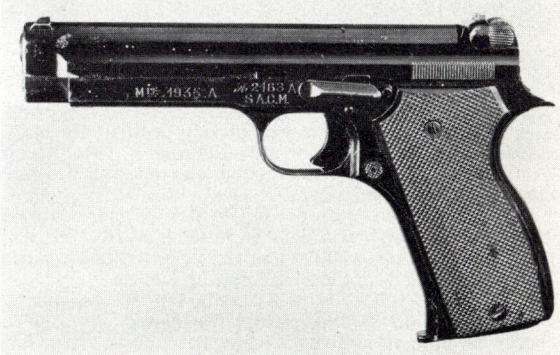

7.65mm SAGEM/SACM M1935A pistol *(RSAF)*.

GERMANY

In the 1890s the Berlin firm of Ludwig Loewe began manufacture of a pistol designed by Hugo Borchardt which was the forerunner of the famous Luger. Loewe ceased production of the Borchardt in 1899, a year after George Luger's design had gone into production with Deutsch Waffen und Munitionsfabriken (DWM). First adopted by the Swiss in 1900 and by the Germans in 1904 the Luger has been made in many places and in very large numbers. Current manufacture is by Mauser-Werke GmbH, Oberndorf-Neckar, where the famous Mauser range of pistols began in 1896 and production of the modern HSc weapon still continues.

Pistols made by J. P. Sauer und Sohn at Suhl and by Carl Walther Waffenfabrik at Ulm-Donau were also in military service before the First World War. The last of the Sauer-designed military pistols was the 1938 model; but Walther pistols are still produced and in service in West Germany and elsewhere. A SIG-Sauer arrangement is described in the entry for Switzerland: the pistols are made at the new Sauer works at Eckenforde.

Following the disruption of the German arms industry in 1945 a new weapon manufacturer, Heckler and Koch GmbH of Oberndorf-Neckar, was set up in 1948 and is producing a substantial range of weapons including pistols.

German sub-machine guns — notably the 'Schmeisser' — became famous during the Second World War. The original and only genuine Schmeisser design was made by Theodore Bergmann at Suhl before the war; and the famous weapon — in fact designed by Heinrich Vollmer — was made by Erma-Werke at Erfurt: Erma remained in the SMG business from 1938 until 1961 with a break between the overrunning

7.65mm Borchardt pistol with shoulder stock *(RSAF)*.

7.65mm Sauer Model 13 *(RSAF)*.

216

of their factory by the Russians until production was recommenced at Dachau in 1951. They abandoned SMG activities in 1961 following a series of unsuccessful ventures.

Mauser-Werke made copies of the British Sten gun during the war; and in the late 1950s produced four new types, two derived from Finnish designs, one taken over from Erma and redesigned and a fourth an in-house design by Vorgrimmler (who had rejoined the company after fleeing to Spain at the end of the war) and Kimmick. Currently-produced German SMG, however, are made by Carl Walther and by Heckler and Koch.

9mm Schmeisser-designed MP18.1 SMG *(RMCS)*.

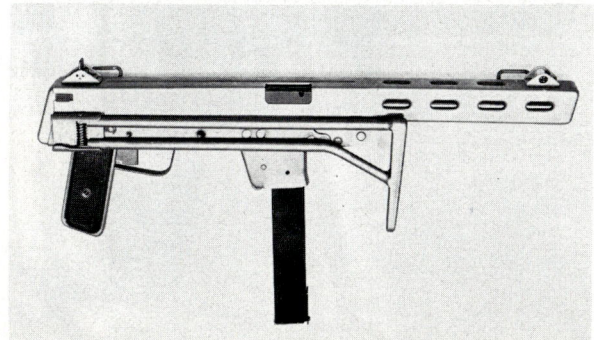

Erma's last SMG — the 9mm MP64.

7.65mm Walther Model 4 (1910) pistol *(RSAF)*.

HUNGARY

Weapons for Hungarian forces are of course now made in state-controlled arsenals and the current Hungarian service pistol, the M48, is a locally-made copy of the Russian TT-33. Hungary has a long tradition of arms manufacture, however, and pre-war pistols made by Fegyvergyan in Budapest are still to be found.

A pre-war SMG was the M39 which was followed during the war by the much modified M43. Both were made by Danuvia in Budapest. Weapons made since the Russian takeover are the M48 copy of the Russian PPSh-41 and the sub-machine gun variant of the AKM assault rifle. This gas-operated weapon is not described in this book.

Hungarian 9mm M39 SMG *(RMCS)*.

Frommer Stop M19 (Fegyvergyan) 7.65mm pistol *(RSAF)*.

218

For some years now India has been developing its capacity for weapon manufacture, mainly by taking production licences from European and North American manufacturers for weapons that have previously been tried in the Indian forces. One such weapon is the British Sterling SMG (Mk 4) of which several thousands were purchased from the UK but which is now made in India.

Although the various campaigns fought in, by and around Indonesia in recent decades have left an extensive range of pistols, sub-machine guns and other weapons in the country, there is only one pistol currently being manufactured there. This is the 9 mm FN Browning HP which is being made at the Ordnance Factory at Pindad.

During the British-Indonesian confrontation in 1963 several types of copy SMG produced in Indonesia were encountered, including weapons of the Beretta, Carl Gustav and Star designs. More recently, however, a locally-designed SMG, the 9 mm PM, was produced by Pabrik Sendjata Dan Mesiu, Bandung. It is no longer manufactured but still in use.

IRAN

No military pistols or SMG are currently manufactured in Iran. Starting in 1943, however, the Russian PPSh-41 SMG was made at the Mosalsalsasi factory, near Teheran, and was known as the Model 22. These weapons were supplied to Russia; but after the war a 9 mm version was produced for a time for the Iranian Army. Subsequently SMG were purchased from the USA and the current weapon is the Israeli Uzi made under licence by FN in Belgium.

ISRAEL

Although a revolver based on the .38 Smith and Wesson was made for a time by the Workers Industry for Arms, no self-loading pistol has yet been produced in Israel and the current weapon is the M51 Beretta which, conveniently, has also been a standard Egyptian weapon.

What Israel lacks in pistol manufacture, however, has been more than compensated by the success of the Uzi SMG made by Israeli Military Industries at Tel Aviv and under licence by FN in Belgium. It is in service in Germany (BRD), Iran and Venezuela as well as in Israel.

Italy's best-known pistol manufacturer, Pietro Beretta SpA of Brescia, has a history extending over three hundred years or more; since Pietro Beretta de Lodovico was following a family tradition when he founded his barrel shop in 1680. Currently in service are the M51, which is also used by Israel and Egypt, and the earlier M34.

Earlier in this century, pistols made by Glisenti at Brescia and Torino were in Italian Army service and may still be encountered in former Italian overseas possessions. The 10.35 mm M1889, for example, was used both in the Abyssinian campaign and in the Second World War. Another Glisenti pistol was the 9 mm weapon originally manufactured by Metallurgica Bresciano Tampini in 1905 and subsequently taken over by Societa Siderugica Glisenti at Torino.

Some early SMG, including the first to go into service anywhere, were made by Officine di Villar Perosa where the 9 mm 'VP' was designed — originally for aircraft use — in 1915. It was subsequently manufactured by Fiat and by the Canadian General Electric Company in Toronto. Later Villar Perosa (OVP) weapons included SMG used during the Second World War. In parallel with their work, however, Beretta started a programme of SMG development which has run with scarcely any interruption from 1918 to the present day, the latest being the Model 12 which is currently in production and in Italian Army service. It is also made in Indonesia.

Another Italian SMG manufacturer is Luigi Franchi SpA, also of Brescia. The 9 mm LF57 is no longer in production but is still in service with the Italian Navy.

9mm OVP (1920) SMG *(RMCS)*.

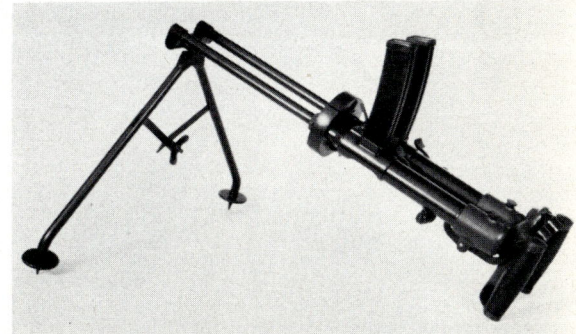

9mm Villar Perosa (1915) SMG *(RMCS)*.

221

JAPAN

Before the Second World War, the Japanese Army used the 8 mm Nambu Model 1914 pistol which came into service in 1925 and was the last of a series of pistols of similar design developed by the Kayoba Manufacturing Company Ltd. This pistol remained in service during the war and was joined by the 8 mm Type 94 made in state arsenals. Since the war several pistols have been developed by Shin Chuo Kogyo (SCK), Tokyo, but they have not been taken into military service. Some are used by police forces.

An 8 mm SMG (Type 100) was made at the Ngoya Arsenal during the war but was not very successful; and an improved (1944) version came too late for extensive service use. The current Japanese Army weapon is a 9 mm weapon designed and made by SCK and introduced in 1960. It is still in production.

8mm Nambu Model 1914 pistol.

Japanese 9mm Type 100 SMG.

222

LUXEMBOURG

A sub-machine gun, known as the Sola Model Super, was produced by the Societé Luxembourgeoise d'Armes SA at Ettelbruck in 1954. Neither it nor a subsequent 'Light Model' was a great success but a few were sold to countries in North Africa and South America.

MEXICO

Although US Colt pistols are used by first-line Mexican troops the .45 Obregon pistol is still in service. This was made by the Fabrica de Armas, Mexico City, but has not been produced for some years.

A sub-machine gun, the HM-3, designed by Productos Mendoza is in production.

NORWAY

Prior to the First World War the Norwegian Army used the Belgian Nagant revolver, but in 1914 the Colt M1911 self-loading pistol was adopted. Initial supplies were purchased from the USA after which the pistol was made at the government weapons factory at Kongsberg until the middle of the Second World War. The pistol is still a standard Norwegian weapon but recent supplies have been purchased from the USA.

POLAND

From 1935 until the Germans overran the country, the standard Polish Army pistol was the 9 mm Radom M35 by Fabryka Broni Radom. From 1940 until the end of the war the same pistol was made at Radom under German control. Current production is, of course, state-controlled and anonymous but the Poles evidently still have a thriving arms industry.

Current SMG production is of the Russian PPS-43. There was a pre-war SMG, designed by the team which designed the Radom pistol, but only a few were produced before the German invasion. It was known as the MORS Model 1939.

Polish 7.62mm 1943/52 SMG.

Pistols for the Portuguese forces have always been imported and for many years, while their requirements were small, they also made do with imported SMG. In 1948, however, a need for enlarged and continuing supplies was met by the introduction of the FBP M48, manufactured by Fabrica de Braco de Prato, which is still a current if somewhat elderly weapon.

A sub-machine gun, designed by Leopold Jaska, was manufactured by the Cugir Arsenal in Romania from 1941 to 1944. Known as the Orita M41 it was used by Romanian troops in the 1941 invasion of the USSR. It remained in first-line service until Romania was absorbed by the Warsaw Pact alliance after which it was relegated to militia and police use.

SPAIN

There has long been a flourishing small-arms industry in Spain and pistol manufacture has been one of its most energetically-pursued activities. The earliest self-loading pistol design originated with Count Giro around 1904 and in 1914 the Spanish Army adopted the Campo Giro Model 1913. The manufacturing contract was given to Esperanza y Unceta of Guernica, who had been founded in 1908 at Eibar as Pedro Unceta y Juan Esperanza and who registered the name Astra in 1914. In subsequent troubled years the company's manufacturing name was changed to Unceta y Compania, Astra-Union and Astra Unceta y Cia who now make the Astra range of pistols.

Another pistol manufacturer was Gabilondo y Cia of Elgoibor who made the Llama series of Colt copies. The pistol currently in service in Spain is the 9 mm Super Star made by Bonifacio Echeverria SA at Eibar who are also manufacturers of the post-war Star range of SMG. Current weapons are the Z62 and Z70/B. Prior to this range the only indigenous SMG had been the Labora made by Industrio de Guerra de Cataluna during the Civil War; other Civil War weapons having been copies of German SMG.

9mm Labora SMG *(RSAF)*.

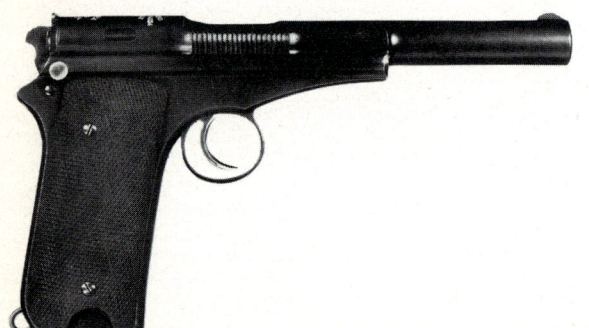

Campo Giro M1913 pistol *(J. E. Smith)*.

Until the Second World War, pistols for the Swedish forces were imported from Russia (revolvers) Belgium and Germany. The 9 mm M40 pistol, however, was a copy of the Finnish Lahti manufactured by Husqvarna Vapenfabrik AB in Sweden; and although production has now ceased the weapon remains in service. The Husqvarna plant has now ceased weapon manufacture; but it may be noted that they were also responsible for making the Model 37-39 SMG which was a modified version of the Finnish Suomi Model 31.

Current SMG manufacture is by the state armament factory Carl Gustav Stads Gevarfactori at Eskilstuna. The M45B weapon is in service with Egyptian, Indonesian and Swedish forces.

SWITZERLAND

A double-action revolver, dating from the end of the last century, remained in Swiss Army service until shortly before the beginning of the Second World War; but in parallel with this the Luger self-loading pistol, which the Swiss were the first to adopt, was in first-line service until 1949. To begin with the weapons were imported from Germany; but from 1929 a slightly modified version was produced by Waffenfabrik Bern and some of these pistols are still in reserve service. The current first-line pistol, however, is made by SIG — Schweizerische Industrie Gesellschaft — which has been making small arms since 1860 and which entered the pistol business by taking up Charles Petter's patents from the French firm SACM — Sociétè Alsacienne de Constructions Mécaniques — but produced only small quantities of the first range of weapons.

Much more success has attended the P210 pistol and its derivatives, of which the M49 service pistol is one. Manufactured at the SIG plant at Neuhausen am Rheinfalls it is in service with Danish as well as Swiss forces.

Recently, because of the official restrictions on direct arms exports from Switzerland, SIG have made an arrangement with J.P. Sauer und Sohn, at Eckenforde in Germany, whereby the latter manufacture a range of SIG-Sauer pistols, designed by SIG, for world-wide sale.

Petter pistol produced by SIG.

A copy of the Walther PP pistol, with only minor modifications, is made by MKE — Makina ve Kimya Endustrisi Kurumu — at Kirikkale, Ankara. It is in service with the Turkish Army.

When US-Turkish relations were strained, at the time of the Turkish invasion of Cyprus, and American arms supplies were cut off, the Turks talked of expanding their arms manufacturing industry. They may yet do so.

A small-arms industry was set up in Egypt shortly after the country attained full independence; and although the main armament of the Egyptian Army is of Russian origin, some SMG made in Egypt are in reserve service. Two weapons have been made: one is a copy of the American Thompson SMG which was made on a small scale with component assistance from the USA: the other is a close copy of the Swedish Carl Gustav M45B. The latter, known as the 'Port Said', was made in some quantity and was certainly used during the 1973 war.

It is likely that future small-arms production for Egyptian forces will be covered by joint manufacturing arrangements with other Arab countries.

UNITED KINGDOM

British military pistols have a long history, but those that are of sufficiently recent manufacture to be likely to be encountered today are the Webley and Webley-derived weapons which were made at various times by Webley and Scott Ltd. in Birmingham and by the Royal Small Arms Factory (RSAF) at Enfield with, as a wartime measure, the support of Albion Motors, Glasgow, and the Singer Sewing Machine Co., Clydebank. The current weapon, however, is the FN Browning HP.

British sub-machine gun history began with the Lanchester, a copy of the German MP28 made by the Sterling Armament Co. at Dagenham. Early production quantities were taken by the Royal Navy but neither of the two versions of this weapon was a great success. An enormous success, however, was scored by the Sten family of weapons, the first of which was developed and produced in 1941, which were manufactured in great numbers by the Birmingham Small Arms Co. at Tysely, the Royal Ordnance Factory at Fazackerley and by the Long Branch Arsenal in Canada.

In the post-war years a most successful range of weapons has come from the Sterling factory and their Mk 4 is currently the British Army weapon (as the L2A3) and has been sold all over the world. It is manufactured both by Sterling and by RSAF in the UK and under licence in India.

9mm Lanchester Mk 1 SMG *(RMCS)*.

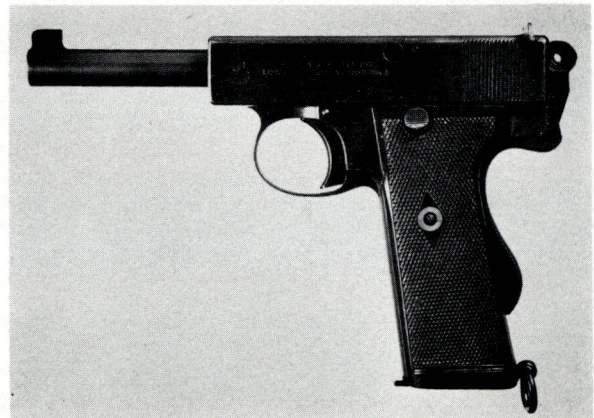

SL .455 Mark 1 pistol *(RSAF)*.

230

Anything approaching a detailed survey of the US small-arms industry would take up far more space than would be reasonable here. The principal manufacturers of military pistols, however, are Colt's Patent Firearms Co., Hertford, Conn; Ithaca Gun Co., Ithaca, NY; Remington Rand Inc., Syracuse, NY; Springfield Armoury, Springfield, Mass; Union Switch & Signal Co., Swissvale, Penn., all of whom have made the Colt 1911 and its variants; and Smith and Wesson Arms Co., Springfield, Mass., who with Colt are long-established military revolver manufacturers. Another manufacturer of military-quality revolvers is Sturm Ruger & Co. Inc., Southport, Conn. Of the self-loading pistols the best-known and most widely manufactured and copied series has been the Colt M1911. It is still in service but the smaller-calibre (9 mm) 1971 model is a possible successor.

There is a similarly formidable range of SMG manufacturers. Auto Ordnance Corporation, Bridgeport, Conn. and the Savage Arms Co., Westfield, Mass., made the Thompson SMG; the M2 designed early in the Second World War was not a success; but a few were made by General Motors Corporation whose Guide Lamp Division, Anderson, Indiana, were the principal wartime manufacturer of the successful M3 and M3A1 designs. The M3A1 was also made by the Ithaca Gun Co. during the Korean War. Manufacturers and developers of SMG designed in recent years include Defence Systems International Inc., Powder Springs, Georgia (Atchisson designs) and the Military Armament Corporation (MAC), also of Powder Springs, for the Ingram SMG.

Colt calibre .45 M1917 revolver pistol *(US Army)*.

YUGOSLAVIA

Pistols for Yugoslav forces are currently made in the state arsenals; but there are also many imported weapons still in service.

Crvena Zastava in Kragujavac made two types of SMG. One, the M49, was copied with extensive modifications from the Russian PPSh-41: the other was designed completely in Yugoslavia — but using ideas from elsewhere — and is known as the M56. Production has ceased but both weapons remain in service.

INDEX

236